Children: Hostages of the State

INNOCENT PRISONERS WITHOUT A TRIAL

WILLIAM D. ANDREWS

Order this book online at www.trafford.com
or email orders@trafford.com

Most Trafford titles are also available at major online book retailers.

Printed in the United States of America.

ISBN: 978-1-4269-5128-2 (sc)

Trafford rev. 02/03/2011

 www.trafford.com

North America & international
toll-free: 1 888 232 4444 (USA & Canada)
phone: 250 383 6864 ♦ fax: 812 355 4082

CHILDREN
HOSTAGE OF THE STATE
INNOCENT PRISONERS WITHOUT TRIAL
WILLIAM D. ANDREWS

Hostage of the State is a product of thirty-four years of working with children both inside and outside the non-juvenile system in several states. It is an inside look at Foster Care, Adoptions and out of home placement of children. It shows a pattern of a County, State and Government control of children, which seems to be out of control according to Constitutional Law and the actual practices.

This is a message to every parent with a child in Foster Care or County, City, State or Government custody. It shows that the removal of many children from their homes is illegal per Constitutional Civil Rights. Civil rights violations carry a mandatory investigation. William D. Andrews lists a few of the most often violated areas he has seen. He points to the Adoption Practice, which often appears to be open fraud. The Adoption Families, Social Workers, and Judges often appeared to be in a Tailor-made Adoption Partnership. He vowed that the practice of removing children from homes without proper application of the law would be stopped. Sexual abuse, threats, lies, injustice, drugs, with physical and verbal abuse were often present. Andrews noted several cases and was in the process of completing this book as an informational novel based on true facts when his own children became involved in the system through divorce. He decided to change the writing slightly. It has been written with the original story as intended. It has also been documented to show the total anarchy of the system.The most fearful thing in the process to Andrews has always been the total shutdown of the voice of both the children and the parents. The total rejection of both children and parental rights that are given as Civil Rights under the Constitution of The United States of America is a tragedy. Literally, every parent who came to Andrews for counsel had no idea of what they could or could not do as a parent. Social Service contact about their children usually left them upset, angry and confused about any direction they could take. They heard only the words of the Social Worker. Many times

this word was so contradictory; they could neither trust nor follow their directions.

As you read, see how easy it is for your child to become a prisoner with no crime and no voice and you," a parent," with no child. You will read a story, a practice and a threat that is fully operational in America. <u>The cases are real. Adjust the system. Deliver and protect your children.</u>

ABOUT THE AUTHOR

William D. Andrews was born in Gates, Pennsylvania. His family of seventeen children lived in a rundown house, yet his mother still had enough to share with so many others. After graduating from High School, he became a Minister and traveled extensively, emphasizing the training of preachers. His love and compassion for the poor, hopeless, mistreated, hungry, and homeless involved him in countless efforts of help and counseling. He considers himself a servant.

TABLE OF CONTENTS

It started out very small, just a small stream near a mountain top. It stands now, a majestic waterfall, cascading water with a two hundred foot drop. Mary Ann was in total shock when social service arrived at the hospital to claim her newborn baby. Now in another state, another hospital she wondered, is this baby mine or the states? I have never used drugs or profanity. Why will you give my children to a drug user with a drug dealer boyfriend? To violate our rights violates our children's civil rights. Abuse is still here. Many have forgotten that abuse can be on all sides. No touch of a loved one, no birthday hugs, no mother's kiss and I will see you in the morning. Truth paints only one picture. Every lier seeks to rewrite history. They won't let me punish my daughter but they punish her and put her in juvenile home. Congress stated that children and youth are the most valuable resources of the United States. He will never vote again. He will never hold a state or government job. A voice from prison was speaking freely inside the house. The desire for family freedom inspired the founding fathers. What happens when justice depends on which judge you stand before? When the enforcers of the law becomes the breaker of the law? Truth and justice dies while injustice, lies, bribery, and favoritism rules. Only a parent is capable of having total love and concern for his family. The man that does not provide for his family is worse than an infidel. Behold the thing that I feared has come upon me. The investigator was aware that a drug dealer on probation was living in the home with three minor children along with three other felons. Their charges were, car theft, assault, robbery and drug possession. Ask yourself, why were all complaints ignored and the family member that reported it was advised to never call their office iwht another complaint on that household? Social service awarded that family four foster care children.

Once inside the system, you may be accused, ignored, humiliated, and cut off from all contact with your children and family. A parent without rights is a heritage without rights. A heritage without rights is a nation without rights. The mandate to counsel every child over twelve to choose foster care or adoption above their parents is mandatory brainwashing of any child over twelve. Why have instructions been routinely ignored which originated from Washington D.C. and the Senate? Why was a conversation relayed about the possibility of my chidren being harmed while in your care? Every parent has a constitutional and fundamental right to custody of their children including care, companionship and fellowship with their children. A parent must either abandon the children or forfeit their parental rights to lose children custody. Parental authority is plenary and prevails over the claims of any minor children and any agency. It is a civil rights violation for any parent or child to be denied a major life activity granted under the Constitution of the United States of America. Is a parent guilty when a warehouse stores food in a special dumpster for them to distribute to the poor and needy? (The garbage can dive that fed thousands). Is a parent guilty when he infiltrates a racist social service program supported by the courts and writes a report for the system?

Men at the top are often ignorant of the ground floor activities. Why should a court ordered parenting class that bars blacks be certified. When an infiltrator takes six weeks to infiltrate the program and as punishment when found, the final recommendation was not another three to four month of class but an additional one year. Four additional classes for the infiltrator. (He was a black man that had taught the same lessons to residents of over twenty countries.) The report was written and submitted to the agency. Their recommendation was not enforced. Still it was not forgotten in future activities. No social, state, country, or govt. program has the right to deliberately refuse, hinder, harass, humiliate or misrepresent the facts of ones attendance or participation in any program funded in part with city, county, state or federal funds. Our children are authors, inventors, lawyers and doctors. Let the nation take its foot of their backs. Let them travel freely the road to success. Not in a hearse, ambulance or patrol car, but in a limousine or taxi driven by the program's overseer. (By our government.)

If foster care or out of home placement can keep your child twenty two months. They can have your child for life. Your child can be adopted out, their name changed, social security changed and the record sealed legally. The illegal financial adoption kickbacks, (outside of the system), is enourmous. The two most destructive tools used inside are (One) The Brain Washing of our children, it is mandated after a child reaches twelve nad has not been adopted out or placed. Selected or skilled counselors are assigned to counsel the children to choose or desire to accept foster care or adoption. The parent must be condemned before the child and made the enemy while the system must be portrayed as the good guy that has come to the rescue. (Two) Declare the parent mentally unfit. Both of these practices have been disputed over and over within the ranks of the military but few people have dared speak of it in child care. This is not hard to comprehend when there is a law against disclosure of some information about youth under twelve years old that pass through the system, read, weep and change.

1. WHAT DOES IT MEAN

Four walls and a fence; a visit on the other side of a window. No touch of a loved one; no birthday hugs; no good morning, how was your nighttime? No I will drive you to school today. No going to the mall to get your birthday present. You will sleep in your eight by ten cell. You will eat in your eight by ten cell. You will read in your eight by ten cell. All of your hopes, dreams, ambitions, and desires, have been captured by your eight by ten foot cell. You are now A Hostage Of Your State. You are a rabbit in a pen. You can't roam the open spaces. You can't be a cowboy and say yippee ki yay, get along little doggie. The open spaces don't belong to you anymore. You can't say, Sugar Plum, I will see you after work tonight. Your favorite coffee shop has disappeared. Your weekend skating party has decreased into an eight by ten foot room. You are an adult. A captured adult, A Hostage Held By Your State.

I awoke this morning to an empty pillow.
Somehow, I was hoping it was only a dream.
Was my wife in the kitchen, the children in school?
I don't smell my bacon or my coffee and cream.

Vaguely I remember somewhere in the past,
I used to awake with ambition and a smile.
Now I struggle to face every day,
Each one seems like I am walking the last mile.

Will you, empty wall, show me a little hope?
Window, just once show me more than despair.

And please door, every time you open today,
Let me walk to enjoy the freedom out there.

We can easily look at the prisoner in prison and lament his position. The local jail and street felon is easily looked down upon as a detainee of the prison system. We continually discuss the crime wave throughout our country and the imprisonment consequences. These are usually crime-oriented discussions. *** but *** are the incarcerated always guilty?

Ti Chen, an immigrant from another country was very glad that a native country person became a regular visitor to his house. He thought nothing of the newfound friendship. It was a great joy to have fellowship with a native countryman in a strange new country. Ti Chen's joy was short lived. He never dreamed that the days they studied English together would one day be considered a curse and a trap. He could not even dream of the idea that the kitchen sessions they had cooking native food together while joking and laughing in the kitchen would come back to haunt him.

Ti Chen's friendship with his fellow countryman became a road to prison. He walked a road of deceit, smiling on his way to the gallows, laughing on his way to the stockade, a trusting man about to become a fool. A couple of months later, this happy, smiling man was met by the police upon his arrival home. The charge was spousal abuse. It seems that his wife took a piece of rope and used it to put a bruise around her neck. She told the police that her husband had tried to strangle her with a piece of rope. Was the lie effective? It was good enough to put Ti Chen in prison for three years. Where was the family friend? Actively   living with the ex wife while planning to return to his native country. One wife's lie was all it took to convict an innocent man. Give her a polygraph lie detector test went unheeded. He was considered guilty unless he could prove his innocence. Ti Chen was innocent but he was A Hostage Of The State. It was his word against a lying wife. It could just as well have been a wife's word against a lying spouse.

I am advocating that in every spousal abuse case that a lie detector test be mandatory if requested by one of the participants. *** I am also advocating that in every child custody case a lie detector test be given if requested by either parent. *** I am also advocating that every social worker involved in any case of child placement out of home be subjected to a mandatory lie detector test if either parent requests it. The drive in most disputes is not necessarily to seek truth. It is usually to win the argument. I was not surprised when I questioned a prosecutor about a person's innocence. The statement to me was; my job is to win a conviction not to prove his innocence. He can always appeal.

Truth paints only one picture. It will never change; neither the past, present, nor future. Truth will always say this is the way it was. History will always verify truth. Every liar seeks to rewrite history. Every person that wasn't there becomes a target for the fiction for the day. Lies have rewritten history for many families. Lies have caused many to become Hostages Of The State.

After one year of marriage, a couple was having a little quarrel. My advice when upset or angry is to take a break and discuss the matter when both have cooled down. Go to the store. Buy some ice cream. Eat a hamburger and talk later. The husband went to the store. He bought a couple of items and returned home. He did not find a loving wife in his parking space. Instead he found several police officers in his parking lot ready to arrest him. His wife had called the police charging him with spousal abuse. He found that it was a good time to accept the offer to spend the night at a friend's house rather than spend the night in jail.

Every charge of spousal abuse must be answered but every person in jail with this charge is not guilty. Consider also that with this charge the abuse can be mental as well as physical. It would be wise for every husband to study the Songs Of Solomon. Or write your own verse. To step into marriage is one of the greatest commitments that a man and woman can make before God. It should point to peace, joy, happiness and hope for the rest of their lives. We should always remember that there is a difference between reasoning together and arguing together. One brings peace the other confusion.

You appeared as a dove in the morning light.
To me a symbol of comfort and peace,
Together we face the turmoil's of this life
With the key to bliss, joy, and happiness release

.
I could not do it alone by myself.

3

William D. Andrews

I searched for years to put someone by my side.
I found a gem. Not quite perfect but neither am I.
Together we share love, peace, without our pride.

You are my love forever sweetheart,
You will always be my dove.
You are the gift to unworthy me,
 A wife, a gift from heaven above.

2. YOUR CHILD IS AT RISK

While we focus on the adults, THE CITIES, COUNTIES AND STATES WITH GOVERNMENT APPROVAL ARE QUIETLY REMOVING THOUSANDS OF OUR CHILDREN from our homes. Thousands of these children will be adopted out to strangers never to see their parents again. Others will float from house to house in foster care with a permanent clouded future. Some of these children will be used as human tools simply to pad the payrolls of some county systems.

Your child may one day be used as human fodder for a bureaucratic system that will devastate a parent's authority, destroy a parent controlled family and still call America a freedom loving country. This while squashing the very foundation of America; what is that? The Basic United American Family; The Freedom Of Every Family to live in a society free from the totalitarian control of a government. A country that offers each citizen the right to life liberty and the pursuit of happiness without government control. While preaching freedom around the world, we are neglecting freedom of our own in the foundation of America. The American Family

This desire for family freedom ideas inspired the founding of America. Europe was forsaken and pioneers who sought freedom for their homes, families, ideas, and religions chose America. They braved seen and unseen dangers at the risk of death to establish this God given right. Now in a seemingly secure nation, our freedom is being challenged by a system that invades our homes without warning. A flag is waved that says, American law declares that I can take possession of your family, home, and child and

5

you cannot interfere. You are now my State Hostage. Sound your freedom cry. It will not help.

What about your child? How easily do you think it is for your child to become a Hostage Of The State? <u>No. You do not call it a prison.</u> You call it Human Services. You call it Social Services. You call it Foster Home. You call it out of Home Placement. No matter what name you give it, it still means that your children are out of your home and their life is being shaped by the State or Government. Someone else will put your child to bed tonight. The child will not get a good night kiss from mother. The child will not tell a sister or brother goodnight. Strangers now control your home with Government approval. You have no rights within your own family. Have you failed as a parent? No! Your new parent is the State Controlled System. It was installed with Government approval. <u>You have not failed. You have been replaced.</u>

Can you protest? Can you ask that an error be corrected? Yes, you can. However in the next six months to a year while reviewing your claims, they have time to reprogram your child. You will not get back a child that you knew, but a child with a cancer that says my parent is now a stranger. Six months of training outside your home, one year of training by a teacher you don't know and now a cancerous tumor in your child that may one day kill parental influence and turn a child into a confused derelict without a positive direction. No longer a favorite son or daughter but now A Hostage Of The State

When did this hostage thing begin? I don't really know. I guess that it was a gradual thing. I can't imagine a state claiming authority over your child in one swoop with government approval or should I say with the Federal Government looking the other way. I understand that it began sometime before I started school. I do remember some things along the way but they are sporadic and do not always deal with my personal imprisonment. I know that I was a little dull and naïve. <u>I just could not imagine the extent of prison or should I say Out Of Home Hostage Life.</u>

I remember complaining when California had a building boom in prisons and a drought in school construction. I became deeply disturbed when I found out that over two hundred fifty thousand children are missing in America every year. Anger really took over when I heard that open slave trade was going on in an island and the U.N. was monitoring, not stopping the situation. When I heard that many of these ended up as slaves in The Middle East, my U.N. Faith hit rock bottom. Could any thing be worse? *** yes *** yes *** yes *** your children being held as Legal Hostages in America.

Is there really such a thing in America today?
An innocent child in a Legal Hostage situation?
I did not know that such things exist.
Certainly not in this great freedom loving nation.

This shocking truth was much too harsh
For my naïve, peace loving eyes.
For a moment, my faith in America faltered,
Still life went on and I a little more wise.

If the politicians knew of our children hostages,
Would their eyes be filled with tears?
Would they ignore the strength of our nation,
And let children perish according to our fears?

An innocent child needs protection.
Too often the child is used as a tool.
A parent should be there to love and protect.
Let no man seek to make parent or child a fool.

3. THE SHOCKING TRUTH OF KNOWLEDGE

I remember Denise who came into our church to talk to the pastor. Denise was sixteen years old and partially blind. She was slightly retarded. Denise walked with a white cane but managed to get around town very well. One of the women counselors took Denise under her wing and became quite a companion in shopping with and escorting her around town. Denise found the new life very inspiring and made a commitment to serve the Lord Jesus. She was filled with the spirit and one of the men baptized her. A few days later, Denise and her counselor made an appointment with the pastor. As a trainee in counseling, this was the first major shock I had ever received in this area of out of home care. Thirty years later, I am still getting shocks but this first one; I don't think I will ever forget.

To the pastor's horror, he found that Denise was living in a home operated by a man and his companion. Denise was abused sexually on a regular basis. The Welfare and Social Services of that city were contacted. They refused to move Denise to another home and their only remedy was to provide birth control pills and demand that Denise take them as prescribed. The provider continued to function as before. Nothing was changed. To add insult to injury, another teenage girl from the same home was brought to the pastor's church with the same complaint. The Social Services and appropriate officials were again notified with the same results. She was given birth control pills and was not moved. These girls were Hostages Of The State System.

The incidents were reported. They were not corrected. Why were they not corrected? This was not a prison of walls. It was a prison of a system. How can such a system exist in America where the world flocks to our door of liberty and freedom? What will they say when they find that a system designed to help one advance and survive has been commandeered like a pirate ship? It is being used to keep a slightly retarded, half blind child in bondage? Denise was not a criminal. She was A Hostage Of The State, an Out Of Home Placement Child. Her church counselor did help secure her another home but what about others facing the same situation or similar situations? Will they be set free or remain bound A Hostage Of The State? <u>Who will listen to a half blind, slightly retarded sixteen-year old hostage?</u>

Because someone with knowledge of the situation came to the forefront, Denise was able to move on in her life as a normal handicapped teenager. The system was no longer to her a forest of negative principles. But it became a highway that she could travel. The Hostage Of The State had a little more freedom. If outside intervention had not persisted when it was rejected by the system, the outcome of this disaster could have been not just shameful but also a horribly tragic lifetime event.

One of the major problems with outside intervention is that it is often recommended by a person employed by a system with no knowledge of the family. During a family separation, a therapist recommended that a big brother system be used in the return home program. During the Out Of Home Placement that had lasted for two years. The therapist was not aware that the boys were a constant companion of their father while in the home. Her recommendation was not help but a divisive force in the home if implemented.

The therapist report stated that the children were not able or willing to confide in the father while in the home. The truth was that he was the only one they did confide in. The lies they told were to the mother because she had another life and any betrayal by the boys was always punished by mother. The therapist diagnosed and recommended per her education and bias while The Pastor and counselor prior and during the divorce were totally ignored as a credible witness. The therapist was accepted because she was A Human Services employee. The Pastor and regular counselor were rejected though they had the ongoing knowledge.

9

The Pastor himself felt that his witness was ignored due to his religious beliefs which the wife injected in her effort to gain custody of the children. The religious belief in question was that the father's minor children should accompany the family to church on a regular basis. Both the counselor and The Pastor agreed with the father at that time. In this case the wife did gain custody in spite of a drug use history and a drug- selling boyfriend. This problem eventually led to Out Of Home Placement. The father spent several months and several thousand dollars in his efforts to retrieve his children from The State Hostage situation.

Tears came to my eyes often as I reviewed the father's paperwork and the counsel that the pastor stated had been given throughout the course of the family dispute and separation. Until today, I have never forgotten the one time that I saw the children briefly after they were put in a Foster Home. They did not look like the children that I saw singing in the children's Christmas Play. Their expression had changed from vibrant joy and enthusiasm to a passive here I am. I don't know what is next? Their confidence was turned to doubt. Fear had set in. Their measure of hope was only, I don't know; I can't plan; as they waved hi to me, a visitor to their church several times. The expression on their face seemed to mirror guilt and condemnation as though they were saying, I am guilty of something, but I don't know what it is. Many months later their looks on that day still bring me to tears. It makes me feel guilty that I could not have delivered them back to a loving parent that day. Sadly, these children had become Hostages Of The State.

Ketouri was twenty -seven years old. She was going through a divorce and accepted her mother's offer to help her out by keeping her three children for a while. Her husband had stopped paying child support and Ketouri thought her mother's offer to keep her children for a while was a great idea. I totally agreed with her at that time. Three years later Ketouri came in seeking counsel again. This time it was on how to get her children back. Her mother had become used to the monthly paycheck. Mother was now fighting to keep the children and Ketouri was on the losing end of a custody battle. The major charge was abandoning the children. During this particular custody fight, I made it a point to find out why there was a favor shown to the grand mother as opposed to her qualified daughter, the mother of the children.

I was amazed to find that at this time the county received about forty five hundred dollars a month for the childcare. Later this was increased to around Six Thousand Dollars a month. This county revenue did decrease later on but this was an eye opener to me. I no longer wonder why your child and mine could be so readily removed from our custody. It was money, honey. Flexing money muscle made the county grab a hostage at any opportunity. This money was paid to the county each month for the care of the children.

While the county was being paid several thousand dollars for each child in its custody, the caretaker was only paid a little over three hundred dollars a month at that time. The rest of that money greased the palms of that county. That mother's children were being used as a hostage to pay the county. I call it legal kidnapping by the city, the county or the state. In a regular kidnapping, you would be asking for ransom. In a legal hostage situation, they are asking for the fee for a Legal Hostage. The money was paid as long as the child was removed from the parent's custody. It was easier for a parent to swallow if the child was in the care of a relative.

I now understood why the parents were always asked if they had a relative that would take the children. Yet ask yourself the question. Is this case putting my child under better loving care or is it a bottled eat, drink, sleep within another persons house and we still control you? Your four walls and a fence just take on a different look. Your children are still locked in. They are still A Hostage Of The State. They are not free. You cannot hug your child every morning. You cannot instruct them to do their homework. You cannot listen to their hopes and dreams. You are a parent without the ability or authority to instruct your child about their clothes, or brushing their teeth. Can you teach them how to tie their shoe or how to fix their bike? Not unless they are in your care, in your home, in their bed. It is a parent's desire to put their ideas, dreams, and ambitions before their child and hope they embrace at least some of them. Parents want their child to seek their advice on some things if it is just, how does this picture look? To us it looks like scribbling but to him it is a tree, to parents, it may be baby sister. What is it to A Hostage Of The State? Ketouri never returned to give me the final result of her efforts to get her children back. But why should a grand mother unite with a state to hold your children hostage over a monthly paycheck? Why should a state permit such a concocted case to hold your child A Hostage Of The State?

11

Where oh where has my child fled?
I tucked her in bed last night.
I kissed her cheek. And straightened her hair,
But today she has fled from my sight.

What did you say my eagle in the sky?
Her running away is not what it was?
How do you know? Where is your proof?
The bumblebee told you by his buzz!

You mean while I slept a policeman came?
He said I, the mother. Was a bad girl.
He took my child to raise in his home?
Now the truth begins to unfurl.

Abuse is still here. Yet many of us have forgotten that abuse can be on all sides; the city, county, state and the family are often abusers. Too often the family is the loser and the children are the sufferers for life because the officials hold the power and authority.

A dictator is usually pictured as one man welding the absolute power over a nation, province, or area. Dictators have not always usurped power. They have sometimes been elected by the people. In the world today, there are some governments that do exercise major elements of a dictatorship. Example *** no voting rights for women *** no government sanctioned schooling for women ***this is government control over a family member. There are consequences when the government controls a child.

Maciana was enrolled in a parenting class. His fourteen- year old daughter had been removed from his home. He was charged with child abuse. His statement*** in my country children must obey the parents. I have a curfew in my home. When my daughter refused to obey me she called the police. The police have a curfew. When she refused to obey their curfew, they put her in a Foster Home. She run away, they make her a juvenile person. They wont let me punish her but they do. Where is the logic? I think I better know how to raise my daughter. His daughter is now A Hostage Of The State and so is he. If parental rights are terminated, who guides a child?

Parents must guide a child in the way he should go.
A child is an empty vessel waiting to be filled.
Many offers are extended with here am I, let me.
Only a loving parent can say to this one yield.

Who plans for the high school prom?
The same parent that took you to first grade.
You remember the child's first set of glasses?
You remember how much you paid?

You will always be the child's mom and dad.
They will always be your children.
Steps will grow feeble and hair will turn gray,
Yet no circumstance can change parent and child.

4.CIVIL RIGHTS NEW FRONTLINE BATTLEGROUND * FAMILY

During the sixties era, America was involved in quite a struggle in civil rights. The emphasis was on equal treatment in schools, jobs, voting voice, use of public facilities, higher education. Just plain equal rights.

Today <u>one of the most violated civil rights in America</u> is Out Of Home Placement of our children. The failure to keep A United Family and failure to Reunite A Family is routinely broken every day by courts in dealing with our children. The most protective cover to this devastating and family-destroying practice in America by the court system is these words spoken often in the courts. <u>We have no authority over the Family Court. The Family Court supersedes. The Family Court decision cannot be interfered with or overruled. Was the decision made in the divorce court? Has another court made a ruling about the children?</u> In other words, unless you have deep pockets or a rich uncle with much money, you have no recourse. Right or wrong if a decision has been made it is final. Take the court decision or the presiding judge ruling and let your family be a silent puppet. ** <u>no!</u> ** <u>not so, said the founding fathers</u>. We are men and women. ** <u>we should and will fight any practice that destroys the freedom of our homes and families.</u> **

In the sixties era, the nation was ignited over civil rights. The focus was on voting, use of public utilities, schools, education, jobs, etc. Most of us are not aware <u>that the basic statement of The Civil Rights Code and</u>

The Human Service Code and The Social Service Code that affects our children emphasis a United Family. Every effort is to be made to keep The Family Together and to reunite The Family if it is separated. This is The Civil Rights and Family Code.

12301 of The Civil Rights Findings Of Congress states that children and youth are inherently the most valuable resource of the United States. The welfare, protection, healthy development, and positive role of children and youth in society are essential to the United States. Children and youth deserve love, respect, and guidance, as well as good health, shelter, food, education, productive employment opportunities, and preparation for responsible participation in community life. Children and youth have increasing opportunities to participate in the decisions that affect their lives. The family is the primary caregiver and source of social learning and must be supported and strengthened.

The Human Services Administrator on Federal Government level, funds every state and county with the stipulation and mandate that every effort is to be made to unite or reunite a family before placing a child in Out Of Home Foster Care,

Every Social Service Agency faces this mandate in order to receive federal funds. Families must remain in home. They must remain united or be reunited if at all possible. Out Of Home Placement is supposed to be the last possible resort. Why is it that the last possible date to receive aid for a particular case is so often met? Is there ever an early end? ** or is there ** any way to collect more funds? This is Hostage Of The State manipulation

Some of The Social Service personnel and Human Resource personnel have become experts at word manipulation and putting speculation on paper. Because of this practice, I recommend that a mandatory lie detector test be given the involved agency workers if requested by either of the affected parents or guardians. *** example *** a mother was taken to a hospital for a swollen jaw. The worker said the jaw looked like possible spousal abuse. It was a tooth cavity, but the judge heard only spousal abuse. The husband was charged as such *** a child said yes when I am bad, to the question does your parents punish you? The report said the child reports fear of physical discipline. The judge heard fear of physical discipline. ***

a child answered a long time ago (it was over 5 years) when asked did your parents ever hit you? It was stated as, the child is afraid to return to his parent. The judge cited fear of the parent.

In two reports from one case, a lesson against drugs and alcohol became mental abuse because the separated spouse said the children associated the lesson with them. Per one social worker report, a child that was taught anyone using drugs is a fool was being taught against one of the parents. These type of reports either on a greater or lesser scale is one of the reasons that I advocate when a person is not able to afford a lawyer they be allowed to choose their own lawyer rather than one appointed by the court. The court should then pay for their lawyer. This would provide a more level ground for children and parents.

Many family courts have assumed a dictator role working under the assumption that they are untouchable. Their decisions are right and accepted because they or their social worker, or other court connected person have said so. A class action review of most out of home placements by Social Services themselves or by The Human Services Commission would make some of our wigs, hairpieces, and natural hair stand on end. The law states very plainly that the goal is to Unite or Reunite The Families. Meanwhile the practice to speedily separate the families is being dished out readily by the courts. America should be due for a passel of family orientated civil rights suits. Both parental and children's civil rights are being violated routinely unless I am reading the codes wrong.

Consider these things ** to violate our child's rights normally violates our family rights, ** to violate our family rights is a civil rights violation. ** to refuse to reunite families as quickly as possible is a violation of both Human and Civil Rights. ** The earliest and not the last possible date is the violation proof date. Otherwise it is a day-by-day violation of Civil Rights. **

Why should a parent have to hire a lawyer for a minimum fee of five thousand dollars to protect their Civil Rights? Family law is not about putting lawyers to work but in putting families together. Provision is made in most courts so a lawyer can be provided if you are not able to afford one. If a lawyer is to be provided, it should be one of the parent's choices.

Consider this. ** I sat in one court case over five times and never heard the lawyer say anything except his name and whom he was supposed to be representing. I sat in another case when the court was in the process of taking a ladies' child from her. The lawyer said nothing through the whole proceedings. When I told the lady what was going on and advised her to tell her lawyer what to do, he approached the bench and asked to be removed. The judge agreed. She assigned another lawyer and on the next session without me present as the ladies advisor, they took her child and gave it to a waiting adoption family. ** <u>I advocate a change in the law that if unable to pay for a lawyer, the parent is allowed to choose the lawyer and the court sanction the chosen lawyer.</u>

Is your court appointed lawyer working for you or the court? Every case is about your total Family Rights. It is not about your children only. A little seven-year-old boy asked to talk to me. He was asked, do you have a brother? He said, I used to have a brother but now he is only my cousin. What a tragedy that Out Of Home Placement has placed that child in such a cross-eyed family fix. What about the grandmother that called from Texas? She had a house that she wanted to give to her grandson. Her question was, where is he?

The system usually makes us think we are not good parents ** most of us should begin asking ourselves first, are my Civil Rights being violated? ** Is there really a reason to remove my children from the home? ** Are one of us parents, if not both really unfit to care for these children in our home? Aren't I the main source of my child's social learning? Why is contact with my child being curbed? Rights are for the purpose of building up, not separating and tearing down the family.

Once upon a time, far across the sea.
The governments our religious freedom curtailed.
A whisper was heard, it came from America.
Then a loud voice. Freedom is here, someone yelled.

Immigrants came, our ancestors too.
The driving force was ** I can and will be free.
Will a government again control our home?
Will my child's joy be decided by the government or me?

We will never cross the sea in droves again,
But we will stand firm in America's free land.
We can pledge to free hostages from the state,
Or as Jefferson, be willing to be hung for our stand.

It is a shame to think that money could influence a county, state, or city agency to take control of a child on frivolous grounds but it can happen. Mary Ann was pregnant and expecting her fourth child when she sought counsel. Mary Ann had decided to leave the city and go to another area to have her baby. After talking to her, it was decided that she had a good reason in her mind.

Several years before Mary Ann had chosen a rather wild life. During that time, she had born two children. At the ages of around two and a half and three years old her children were taken from her. Mary Ann had sought counsel at the time of the removal of her children, but to no avail. One arrest and a charge of prostitution won over her protests. Her children were taken and placed for immediate adoption. They were given to a family that was on the waiting list for adopted children. Mary Ann did make a few changes and adjustments and faced life again in another city.

Mary Ann did return to her hometown after two years. She looked forward to having her third child and raising the baby in her new family setting. Mary Ann thought nothing of going to the hospital to have her third child. However, hospitals have their own unexpected arrivals.

Mary Ann was in total shock when Social Services arrived at the hospital to lay claim to her baby. Her former record made her A Hostage Of The State. Her child was confiscated property. Because the child was under two years old, it was up for immediate adoption. As a matter of coincidence** (of course)**the child was adopted out almost immediately. To whom? That fine family that had been waiting for an infant baby to adopt. Little shocked, reluctant Mary Ann had just made their day. Now what about mother Mary Ann? Mary Ann now had three children that were adopted out per the state order. These are children that she will possibly never see again.

Mary Ann wanted to protect the fourth child. Will she succeed? I don't know. Mary Ann's child is now an unborn fugitive. Social Services,

Human Resources, Welfare Persons, are waiting at the hospital door. This is not Moses in Egypt being hid to save his life. This is a mother trying to keep her child. Her new marriage, her new job, her new city, will it save the child? Her record says that she is A Hostage Of The State and as long as she is in this state, her record makes her a hostage. *** And her unborn child with her. What would you do if your unborn child were considered an unborn prisoner of the state? Civil Rights; where are you?

Mary Ann is one of thousands of mothers that don't know whether they will be able to keep their child or not. Her four years of living a wild life has marked her for the rest of her life. A shadowy memory and a haunting question will stalk every child that she births. Is my baby mine or will this state find a reason to claim my child? As one twenty-one year old girl stated to her counselor; I am sorry, I have to leave this state. I will not let them take my baby again. Do you know what it is like to think that you are having a baby for someone that is waiting in the wings like a vulture on a tree? Someone that wants the status of a parent and the pleasure of marriage but is willing to break the heart of a real mother? A person that won't suffer the pain and anguish of birth. One that won't walk in the summer suffocating with heat. One that won't enjoy the moments of running to the bathroom to throw up their morning breakfast. One that won't have the joy of saying to the husband will you tie my shoe lace? I can't reach them. One that won't have the joy of working out to lose the slight bubbly belly or wonder how to get rid of the stretch marks. This very thought is like a dagger in my heart. Why should a real mother have all the fun while someone waits to take your baby?

Such a statement should make a person do all in their power to never allow their children to become A Hostage Of The State. Every child is a person, not a law or statute. They are flesh and blood, not legislated laws or pawns. Why should they become A Hostage Of The State? They are not checkers to be pushed across the board. They are people, mostly poor people, parents and children being manipulated by a system that guarantees a paycheck from Uncle Sam through the back door of your family. Have you protested your family injustice? Have you filed your Civil Rights Protest? Hurry; file while the fee is free.

Every American is entitled to Civil Rights.
So our Government Constitution has said.

They are obligated to freely investigate.
There is no money-filing fee for you to dread.

Life carries problems from birth to the grave.
Every challenge develops our skills.
As far as our children, their lives we must save,
And program in them an overcoming will.

What if our enemy becomes The System or State?
Can we become guerillas working underground?
In a free society, ** justice ** this would berate.
Our efforts should be to make truth abound.

Cry aloud the standard that all men are free.
Every parent has a right to raise his or her own.
This is the reason families came across the sea;
To make the land of the free their new home.

5. A SLIGHT CASE AGAINST FAMILY DRUG USE

As you read this portion, remember that my personal teaching is that every drug dealer, (not drug user), and every drug trafficker is a serial killer and should be handled as such.

Drug use in the home has continually been one of the most inconsistent factors in child custody cases. It should be mandatory that whenever drug use is involved, the guilty parent should be denied the children. This should be automatic. Drugs produce a mind change that alters normal decision-making patterns. It is possible to become addicted to some drugs just through handling them without gloves. Every child in an environment where illegal drugs are used, sold, or manufactured is subjected to great danger and detrimental lifelong influences.

The following two cases are among the worst two comparisons that I have seen in the last thirty years of monitoring and advising such cases.

Ron was going through a custody battle in a divorce case. His wife was on drugs but she was still given custody of the three children. His wife was picked up and jailed in an unrelated incident. Fortunately Ron was able to pick up the children. Ron arrived in the court and advised the judge that he had the children. He asked the judge for custody and the judge agreed since the mother was in jail.

Mason was not so fortunate. His wife tested positive for drugs but he was advised that children were not removed from the mother for drug use in this county... The mother would be sent to a drug program and if she took the program, she would retain custody of the children. The mother was allowed to retain custody while going through the program. Mason's wife did complete the program. She did retain custody. Unfortunately Mason's children were placed in a home with a drug using mother and a drug-dealing boyfriend. This resulted in mental, physical, and sexual abuse of the children. After charges of drug use, possession, driving under the influence, child endangerment, and other charges over the space of years, the mother still possessed the children.

Mason with a clean criminal record, excellent civic record and security level job had still not been able to obtain possession of his children because they had become Hostages Of The State through the divorce decree. The Family Court decided to give the children to a drug-using mom. After several years, the state finally took the children from the mother. Tragically, rather than give the children to Mason; they put the children in a foster home with the stipulation that if the mother changes they will return them to the mother. This hostage had only two choices, mom or foster home. Why was dad not included? <u>His Civil Rights were violated.</u>

This was a case where Mason often heard the words; we can't go against the Family Court. They made the original decision. Why were the children not given to you? In spite of the factual drug use and the drug related violations of the residents of the home, the children still remained with the mother in this environment. Mason, with a perfectly clear record was always met with a suspicious why were you not originally given the children. The Family Court was never mentioned as a possible wrong decision-maker. The state protected its Hostage Taking despite the ongoing record.

Over the years, Mason watched his children grow. Each child that reached eleven and above became a problematic juvenile. A continuous line of people in and out of the home brought charges of car thefts, armed robbery, thefts, drunkenness, drug possession, driving under the influence, and several other charges to the mother's home address. Still, a wall was put between Mason and the justice system. He presented the police records of the house residents. He presented the deteriorating records of his children in school. As they became juvenile, he protested. It did not work. Every court appearance he appeared in, the court simply stated, we will review the possibilities. A few months later, the same thing; No change. This is Hostage Of The State big time.

This particular case was extremely disturbing to me because Mason had never been given a solid reason on why the children were never entrusted to his care. In spite of a continual history of unfit mother, his wife or former wife still had a target that if she changes, they would return the children to her. These children were Hostages Of The State. <u>Mason watched his children being corrupted with, city; county approval under the guise of the Family Court made the original decision. Mason watched his Civil Rights being violated under the guise of the Family Court made the original decision.</u>

Mason had to be restrained many times through counsel. Yet it was the Family Court and not Mason that refused to face the facts in that particular case. The Federal Law states that every effort is to be made to return a child to a parent before committing a child to a foster home. This facet of the law is being routinely overlooked or should I say being bypassed by Social Services and Courts continuously.

Most of the people don't know the law and if they did know, the poor cannot normally reach into a bank account and pay the lawyer fee to fight the case. <u>The Courts and Social Service for the state often make the children Hostages or Wards of the state under questionable circumstances.</u> They can laugh in the citizen's face if they choose, because we don't know the law. <u>A Hostage Child is a helpless child.</u> Rise up and do every thing you can to preserve the freedom of your child. Direct his life. Don't let four walls become his Hostage Home away from home. <u>No one loves like a father. No one cares like a mother.</u> A foster parent should be the closest thing possible to a real parent imitation.

How do you rate a foster parent?

TO THE FOSTER PARENT

My best foster care parent.*****   they love me as much as their own children *** love your neighbor as yourself.*** it is not just for money *** it is because a need exists *** I will be brother to those that need a brother and a sister to those that need a sister. I will feed the hungry and clothe those in need. If I lend to the poor, The Lord will repay me. It is not hard.

23

This is my family. I don't have much but, you are welcome to what I have. We share as one. I offer you love without strings. Only love to help you live, succeed, and share the same with others. I am a willing, loving, caring foster parent and I care for you.

Children are our heritage. Freedom engrosses our minds. Why should you have to take care of another man or woman's child unless it is an emergency? If that emergency arises, we shall act as a deliverer and not a Hostage Taker. Our pledge is to love, joy, and peace in your home. Our efforts are to fulfill the desires of the parent in helping them to establish a strong, freedom loving American Family.

America represents freedom to the world. God help America when or should this representation ever change. Let us pledge the freedom of a United Family without violation of any Family Rights. Civil Rights begin and ends with your and my family. God blesses a free America. Freedom should begat freedom. Every hill and every valley should ring out with the joyful cries of a free child. The beckoning hand of America should be stretched out to every child. Let them live in a United Family Home and not as hostage in any city, town, or state. <u>Every child belongs in a United Home if possible. Not four walls but a United Family. Not Foster Care but Father, Mother Care.</u>

6. PREPARATION OF THE DELIVERER

Bill woke up struggling to breathe. He had been dreaming that a hand was trying to smother him. He woke up striking out with his hands and gasping for breath. This was a continual dream. It had started right after Bill accepted the call to preach. As long as he could remember, Bill had known that his mission in life was to preach God's word. Bill's early life often reminded him of the prophet Samuel. Everyone that he met or came in contact with as a child seemed to know that he was destined to become a preacher. From the age of six on, the local pastors made it a point to have him accompany them on special trips or on their various evangelistic crusades. His religious life and church attendance floated between the Baptist, Methodist, and Jehovah Witness Assemblies.

Bill was recognized as a morally, religious kid throughout the area. He went to catechism at the local school house because in his area at the time, he could not be a member of the Catholic Church due to local racial prejudice but the churches were allowed to use the local schools in the area during school hours. (How many lawsuits would this practice stir today)? The local Assembly of God Church only welcomed him when they had special events. Bill accepted this in stride. He knew that he eventually would be a preacher but never dreamed or considered anything other than a segregated society. This seems strange today because Bill has never pastored anything but a thoroughly integrated church.

Each of these local church assemblies left a profound effect in Bill's spirit and helped prepare him for the day that he stood as a deliverer to the Hostages. From the Baptists, Bill learned to never close the door on a member. Any prodigal son may one day come back home. When he does return, his father opens the door to all the fullness of his love, joy, peace, mercies, and positions of love and authority that is available. He learned what true forgiveness is. He learned what restoration means. He learned that God still has some Moses, Abrahams, Pauls, Davids, Jacobs, and many others in this day that have erred, fallen, and risen again to do God's work. Bill never accepted the doctrine of once in Christ, never out, but he did accept the doctrine that the door of salvation is never closed as long as life is present. Luke 15;11-32 is one of the principals of Bill's ministry.

Bill learned from the Methodists the value of education and the necessity of remembering to help others achieve similar positions and upward mobility. He learned how not to scorn the lowly but how to lift their hand and expect a miraculous change. John 3;11 we speak that we know and Proverbs 4;7 wisdom is the principal thing; therefore get wisdom; and with all thy getting get understanding are a key part of Bill's ministry.

Bill didn't remember when or how he learned to read or whether or not someone taught him to read. No one in his family or house was capable of teaching him. He did know that when he entered first grade he could read quite well. As part of the only black family in the school, and the only person in first grade that began the grade reading, Bill got a lot of attention. He was periodically taken to all the other rooms and was asked to read for them. Bill was used to the acknowledgements of his limited abilities from his travels with the local pastors and preachers. Yet this recognition was a little different.

The preachers were amazed at his Bible knowledge. The school parade was more of curiosity rather than praise. Where did this ability come from? Is he from outer space? This could not possibly be from a black child. However, only one picture stuck in Bill's mind. He remembered himself standing in the front of the schoolroom reading while his brother sat in a chair in the back of the room, totally ignored. His brother was the only black in his class and they asked him no questions and gave him no help. His brother was segregated inside the room. He was the back seat observer.

He was the boy in a chair. A dunce without a dunce hat. With this picture before his face, Bill vowed a silent vow. Bill vowed that my children would always excel if I have my way. If they fail to excel, it will be because they themselves will it and not society. He vowed to inject this thought of being able to excel in spite of any opposition in every person that would hear. <u>He became convinced that every person has an ability to excel if they can find it or society allows them to pursue it.</u>

Bill's brother never learned to read. He never learned to spell. However, something peculiar happened in Bill's brother's life. His brother began speaking on a level that puzzled and confounded many people that he met or came in contact with. His conversations began sounding like that of a professor. Bill would often have to use a dictionary to interpret the words that his brother used. Still! All the words were correct. How could he use these words if he could not read? Where did he hear the words to learn to use them? He still cannot read. He still cannot spell. He still sounds like a professor. This still remains an educational mystery to those that were raised with him and those around him. Bill's mystery sent him to school reading, writing, and doing arithmetic. Bill's brother's mystery gave him a college level vocabulary without the benefit of a teacher, tutor, or counselor.

The Jehovah Witness taught Bill two things that heavily influenced his ministry. First they were the only group in the area that was integrated. Go into all the world and preach the gospel to every creature was preached as a mission. Matthew 28;19-20 go into the highways and hedges and compel them to come in Luke 14;23 was taught as a mandate and not as an option.

In his years of training preachers and teachers, one of Bill's favorite points was that the Christian Church has never fulfilled its mission to go into all the world. Souls still die while the world waits. American dogs get more attention from the church than lost souls. On the last report that I read about the American Christian Church and its Missionary response, I read that more money is spent on dog food in America than is spent on Missionary efforts to reach the lost.

The Catholic Church helped to center Bill's focus of deliverance. It seemed to Bill that every abused wife and every runaway kid showed up at his house continually during his early years. Bill's mother, with at least eight children of her own in the home at a time, always found room for one more plate of food and one more pallet on the floor. Whether made of old clothes or rags it made a bed for the night. No one was ever turned away. Hobos riding the freight trains often stopped by for a meal. Even some escaped German prisoners found time to stop for a plate of food. This helping the needy became a part of Bill's character. But his character was growing.

At that time, most Catholic Churches in Bill's area had an orphanage. Bill began praying around first grade that a way would be made to help take care of more orphans. His prayer was very simple. Why should only the Catholic Church take care of the children when there are so many orphans especially during war time?

Bill's heart was especially touched at this time to help the weak and helpless. His compassion and prayer for other children became a little treasure chest within his heart. He never forgot, Suffer Little Children to come unto me and forbid them not for such is the Kingdom of Heaven. Mark 14;13-16. As a child Bill became the Good Samaritan for the village and a prayer warrior for small children.

His Good Samaritan role helped as far as the adults were concerned but his neighborhood role changed little as to his youth role. He still had to fight his way to and from school almost daily. Every walk that he took to the store was a walk of faith. Bill said, he didn't walk through a valley of death but he certainly did walk through a hail of rocks often.

In spite of the continual stigma that earned him a good reputation as a good deed person and a terrible reputation as a neighborhood bully, Bill had a tremendous attitude of joy. Many of the adults found it great to talk to him and discuss their problems with him. He was in effect an unqualified, though welcomed in the area, unofficial counselor with a sense of both seriousness and joy among the adults.

The Assemblies Of God Churches at that time were the number one evangelistic church in America as far as reaching out to foreigners. Yet Bill could not become a member of their church in America because of racial prejudice. From this group, he learned the hunger of those that had never heard the gospel. He also learned the importance of raising up their own native missionaries. Our missionaries would go to visit, but their preachers were there to stay. They would live or die before the mirror of their land, their people, and their ministry. We went to preach, mix, visit and come back to the segregation of America.

He learned that our traditions truly do make The Word of God of none effect. He learned that our traditions to the foreigner were accepted for what they were; often church hypocrisy and not true gospel. Our church hour in America was often and still is in some areas of our country, the most segregated hour in the nation. Bill was growing but not just through gospel reading. His experience was growing him for his greater ministry; to fulfill the mission of Christ; to set the captives free. Isaiah 61;1, Luke 4;18

Between the age of six to fourteen while living on the very segregated Mason Dixon Line, Bill made many of his commitments and vows that stayed with him through his entire life. Every Friday was payday. Every Friday, Bill watched as a parade of coal miners jammed his house. They came in with their mistress, and girl friends. Bill knew the neighbors for miles around. It disturbed Bill that so many wives were being neglected while their husbands squandered the paycheck on rowdy women. This disturbed Bill. He made a vow to God that he would never be unfaithful to a wife and would never neglect his children.

Bill's popularity has always made him a suspect from a carnal minded society on whether or not he would be faithful in such a wicked age. One of Bill's general answers was most men and women don't get angry with me because I am wrong but because I won't get wrong.

During this time, Bill also made a vow to never drink. Watching men arrive on Friday night and drink continually until Sunday was considered by the child Bill as a fool's concept of life. Watching men sleep in a corner or on a chair and wake up only to ask for another drink became offensive to Bill but only toward his own drinking. His inborn religious conviction was always that it was an individual's choice. Our duty is not to force or coerce. Our duty is to inform, pray, hope, and persuade if they will listen. The decision is always the individual's own.

Two of the most life forming vows in his entire life occurred during this time. Bill's philosophy, a combination of mother, Bill and experience was to never start a fight but if you do fight, never lose. Being the only black family in the school was a great experience ???? Really ???? No one fought Bill by themselves. Bill often fought five to fifteen kids at a time. (Amazing) Bill never lost. Bill only ran once.

Bill recounts this one experience. He arrived home and advised his mother that this fifth or sixth grader attacked him and he ran. Bill was in the first grade. Bill's mother instructed him. Go and find him right now. You must fight him and not lose. You must win. Bill walked the three miles or so back past the school house. He found where the boy lived and knocked on the door. The boy opened the door. Bill pulled him out and beat him up. Bill's mother had followed Bill but had stayed about a quarter of a mile behind him. No one noticed her until she spoke. When she arrived, Bill had the young man on the ground beating him and the parents were trying to separate them. Leave them alone. She spoke and everyone stopped. All right Bill. That is enough. Bill never ran again. He avoided many incidents but he never ran again during his fighting days.

Around the age of thirteen, Bill vowed to never fight again. It was a vow that he broke three times after. Bill was proud of his 22 rifle and often cleaned and oiled it. Good shooters in that area could strike a match or break a matchstick in two at thirty to fifty yards with a twenty two rifle. Bill was not that good. On this day, a couple of ex-convicts decided to go to Bill's home to do violence. When they came to Bill's home, he loaded the gun and pulled the trigger. The gun did not fire so Bill resorted to his physical attack. After the young men's flight, Bill examined the gun as to why it did not fire. He had cleaned, oiled, and tried the gun the night before. To his surprise, the firing pin was missing. Bill was convinced that God had saved him from prison or a country ku klux klan lynching by removing the firing pin. Bill vowed to quit fighting.

A few days later as Bill walked to the store; a larger group of young men with these same men among them surprised Bill. Bill had a knife in his pocket. He reached in his pocket but could not get it out in time. His Levi Jeans were too tight. Bill got so angry that he literally blacked out. He remembers nothing about that moment. When he came to himself,

he had done so much damage that he decided that he would strive to never again lose his temper and get angry again. This part of Bill has always followed him. It is literally almost impossible to make Bill angry. Bill shows displeasure occasionally but anger is like a moon eclipse. Bill remembers getting angry since that day only once in over forty years. Bill considers this one of his greatest assets in dealing with problems. Still, this characteristic has caused multitudes of accusations that **** you don't care or you are not concerned. Nothing could be farther from the truth. If we believe that the Eternal God is in control and his angels are watching over us, why should we worry?
Let not your heart be troubled. Believe in God.

It was during this same time that Bill decided to never use profanity again. Bill used his last swear word at age fifteen. He was upset at the pay he received for cutting firewood.

Living on the Mason Dixon line had its advantages along with its disadvantages. Total segregation was not practiced but pocket segregation was the order of the day. One of the more comical moments of segregation in this area was to watch some blacks when wanting to stay in a motel or hotel. They would tie a towel on their head and fake an accent while posing as a foreign dignitary. This manner often got them service for a day at a motel or a meal without having to go to the back door of the restaurant for a take out plate.

His early religious experience was great for Bill.
It showed him the value of several denominations.
He learned that only God's word is true.
Men can produce only glossy imitations.

We should believe in Christ as the scriptures say.
It would be harmony, peace and brotherhood.
We would love our neighbor as our selves.
Joy and peace would be ours as Jesus said it could.

Bill would often find himself halfway between being awake and being asleep. At times he could see a hand choking him and at other times he could see himself sleeping and his hands flailing to stop the attack. This time, the attack was so severe and the picture so plain that Bill decided to talk to the pastor. This talk helped convince Bill that one of his missions in this life would be to set those in bondage free. At this time he did not know who, what or when. Yet in his mind, he knew that he had to set the captives free.

7. SUPERNATURAL PREPARATION IN BILL'S LIFE

The pastor told Bill that every person called into the church is born into God's Family. The charge is; go into the vineyard (all the world) and work. Go and destroy the works of the devil. Heal the sick, cast out devils, raise the dead, baptize believers, and open the eyes of the blind while preaching the gospel of Jesus Christ. For the first time in his infant ministry, Bill became aware that he was in a spiritual battle. His enemy was the devil whose main goal was to kill, steal and destroy. Every person that died outside of Christ was a victory for Satan. To die in sin is to perish in hell forever separated from God.

Bill heard for the first time that almost everyone that this pastor had known in the church had similar experiences where they had nearly suffocated after receiving salvation through Jesus Christ. Bill was assured that, even in his dreams, he had power over the devil. No weapon formed against him would prosper. He could bind and cast out that spirit and forbid it to return. He, Bill, was in control and not that spirit.

That day, Bill became aware that he had a mission from God and the devil was determined to stop him. He learned that we are fighting against spirits and not people. His prayer from that day forth became give me faith to always stand and to always win by faith. He now knew that he could not suffocate. God himself breathed into him the breath of life. He did not live by flesh and blood only but by the spirit or Word Of God. Jesus was raised from the dead by God Himself and God Almighty would not suffer any of his children to stay in the grave. He would raise them to live eternally with him. Bill left the pastor session with a new elevation of faith. He would live and not die.

In one of Bill's recurring dreams, Bill was always running from the devil. The bad part of this dream was that he was always running over the pits of hell. He was always extremely fearful because he could look down into hell itself. Bill began immediately trying to take control over this dream and stop the devil from chasing him. In a matter of a few days, Bill had gained complete control of his dreams. He could cast the devil out, bind him, and even heal all the sick in his dreams. Bill, the deliverer was growing. Within Bill's spirit a new surge of power was arising. He could envision this victory in his sleep. He could literally feel the power and would often awake speaking authority over the power of the enemy.

I speak as an oracle of The Mighty God.
Flee back to the darkness from whence you came.
I am now a soldier in the army of God.
I bind your power and cast you out in Jesus name.

Bill now began to attempt to transfer that dream power into day-by-day power. He began following the ministry of several deliverance ministers. His prayer became ** Lord let miracles, signs, and wonders fill my ministry. Periodically, instant healings took place. Bill's focus now became; Lord, if you will deliver every now and then, increase my faith that it will become every time I pray. Yet in the back of his mind, Bill was a very shy young man. He never wanted to be in the forefront or the limelight. He always preferred to be in the background and push others. This made Bill wonder if he could or would be a deliverer to multitudes. This he knew, he would one day be. How? That was the question.

Bill liked to associate himself with King David of The Old Testament. He liked to wander in the woods and sing God's praises. He became a very prolific poet and songster. The writings were always God centered and heavenly directed. He felt a sense of closeness with the lord while wandering in the woods. There was one exception. He was always afraid of snakes.

It was during these times that Bill had one of his least mentioned experiences. An encounter with what he believes were extra terrestrial beings. Several air sightings had occurred in the area that were not fully explainable. Several UFOS were seen in the area followed by jet planes. The objects were of different shapes and one looked as big as a house to those in the village that were watching it. The objects could move in different directions at will; from straight ahead to straight up or an instant right or left direction.

Bill had decided to cut through the woods and take a short cut home this night. He and his cousin had stayed too long in the neighboring town and were about three miles from home. Darkness was just about upon them. It was a much shorter distance if they left the road and cut through the woods. As he walked through the woods with his cousin, they saw a light in the distance and heard a hum like a type of machinery. Bill knew that there were no persons or beings in the area for this was one of his wandering grounds. As he and his cousin approached the light they could see men or beings in what appeared to be some type of white suits. They spoke in a foreign language. The area was surrounded by a white light. Bill and his cousin tried to cross the light but could not get past it. It seemed like a barrier that you could see past but could not get past. The next thing that Bill remembered was he and his cousin approaching the end of their short cut several miles away. Bill checked the area some time later but found no evidence of any person, vehicles, etc. Just the area woods. Bill has never been able to account for the short memory loss. He did not even discuss it with his cousin who is now deceased. This remains one of Bill's mysteries. He refused to speak of this incident for several years.

Though this mystery remains such, there are several supernatural incidents that Bill never forgot. These incidents Bill believes, lifted him into his God given ministry. His reluctance to stand in the forefront was still there but Bill felt that God would somehow erase the shyness and promote a new boldness. It didn't happen. In fact, this is the first time that Bill has spoken of these particular incidents together.

Bill was filled with the Holy Spirit at the age of seventeen years old. He was immediately confronted with the doctrine of fasting and praying. It was Bill's practice to stop by the church every night after work and pray. On this night, he had a question concerning his ministry. He had purposed to pray until the Lord Jesus answered him. As Bill prayed, the building was suddenly filled with a light brighter than the sun. When Bill opened his eyes, he was shocked, frightened, amazed, you name it. As Bill looked around, the pews were dancing. The lights were dancing. The piano and organ were dancing. All the church furniture was dancing as Bill looked up; a light was moving down toward the church at incredible speed. Instinctively Bill knew it was Jesus.

His knees became weak and he could not stand. He fell to his knees and cried stop. Instantly Jesus stopped. Bill asked Jesus a question. Immediately the answer was in Bill's mind. He heard no voice. He could see no image of Jesus. He only saw the brightness of the light and knew that Jesus was in the center of it.

Somewhere during the conversation, Bill asked for Jesus to answer him from the scripture. Instantly Jesus spoke several scriptures into Bill's mind. Bill asked Jesus to slow down so he could write the scriptures down and read them. Jesus spoke again and allowed Bill time to write the scriptures down and read them. Bill did not know how long the session lasted. He did know that a different manner of communication with the lord Jesus began that night and continued for over forty years. Whenever Bill wanted or needed an answer from The Lord, he would ask and Jesus would give him the scriptures which would be a direct answer from the lord. It was like a two-way conversation with Jesus answering from The Bible because that is what it was and is. At the time of this writing Jesus still communicates with Bill in this fashion.

Near the same time, a new manifestation of The Lord Jesus spirit began in Bill's life. Bill was standing on the sidelines while one of the saints related his dream to his brother. The dream's meaning was as clear as crystal to Bill. It was some time later that Bill fully realized that God had given him the interpretation of dreams. God was preparing for himself a deliverer; a worker for Jesus Christ.

We know that our faith will be tried. Our problem is hanging in there until it becomes like pure gold. 1Peter 1;7. Not all of Bill's faith trials came out good. In fact Bill considers himself at the bottom of the scale as to his having faith. One of his more victorious trials was when he was on his way to a conference and his front tire rods became bent. He stopped at three garages to get a price quote. The price he got at each garage was the price of his trip. He had to either cancel the trip or fix the car. Bill decided to pray and ask The Lord Jesus to fix the tire. After prayer, bill took the car back to the same three garages. All three said there was now no problem. Bill went to the meeting. He was confident that God had worked a miracle and straightened out bent steel.

Shortly after, as Bill prepared to leave Chicago, he stopped at a red light. A car made a left hand turn and accelerated heading straight for Bill. All Bill had time to do was say, Jesus! Bill watched the automobile head straight for him and then disappear. The traffic was bumper to bumper. The car could not have gotten through on the left and the sidewalk was on the right. Where did the car go? Only Jesus knows. God was preparing Bill to believe in miracles.

The Lord's Supernatural Voice was just awesome in speaking to Bill. One night Bill was going through what he considered his greatest trial in his ministry up to that time. In Bill's front yard was a tree. That night the tree was half destroyed by storm winds. Bill looked at the tree thinking he would have to cut it down. When he arrived the next afternoon he was shocked to see the tree totally restored. The Lord spoke to Bill that day that he would build, and restore if Bill would only let him move in his life.

Bill related to us another incident in which he believes an angel spoke to him. He was faced with one of the most important decisions of his life at that time. Bill parked his car just after a snowstorm. He walked to minister to a man that had been diagnosed with cancer and walked back to his car. As he neared his vehicle, a man was pacing back and forth on the sidewalk beside his car. Two to three inches of snow was still on the ground. The man had both hands in his pockets and spoke with an accent. As Bill approached, he gave Bill a message which was the specific answer to the decision that he had to make. Bill opened the car door, put his bag in the car and turned around. The man was gone. A six-foot fence was on the left and the street was empty. No one was on the sidewalk. Bill thinks God sent him an angel to give him his answer. God is A Supernatural God. He will never allow a failure or us to be ashamed if we obey him.

It is always fascinating to know that The Creator of The Universe, Almighty God Himself has chosen us to carry His Name and to do His Bidding. Jesus' promise is that he will never leave us or forsake us. When we see this scripture fulfilled in our lives, there are no words to describe it. Bill was driving across country and had to make a stop in Illinois. He had been driving for several days and had become very fatigued. His next stop was several hours away and Bill knew that he could not make the drive. When Bill left his stop in Illinois to get into his car, he said another person got in the car with him. At the time Bill had not slept for three days. He felt two hands being placed on his shoulders. As he drove off, another hand took hold of the steering wheel. Periodically, he could see another person sitting next to him in the front seat. He does not remember any of the drive. He only remembers getting into the car and arriving at his destination in Pennsylvania. He does not remember stopping for gas or anything. He only remembers waking the family upon arrival. Bill believes God's Angels drove his car that night.

The most memorable and lasting supernatural intervention per Bill's report is the one that God sent at the beginning of his evangelistic career. Bill was lying in bed when two angels descended down through his roof and stood at the foot of his bed.

Bill lay on his back watching the angels descend. He was frozen with what he describes as a mixture of fear, astonishment, and the unknown. Bill could feel his hair standing on end as the angels stood there. He saw no visible body but in his mind saw both standing there. One of the angels spoke and said go pray. Bill slept in a small alcove in front of his main bedroom. His bed was his desk and prayer alter. He leaped up and stepped into his prayer room, (bedroom). Before his knees hit the floor, he was immediately entranced in a vision.

A great host of saints were walking toward a great light. The light appeared to be near the bottom right side of the throne of the Lord Jesus. Jesus was sitting on a high throne. A hugh multitude was walking in two lines; a right line and a left line. Bill was at the front in the left line. Directly in front of Bill and coming toward him was a blinding light that he could not see past. When the light got directly before him, a pair of hands presented the light to him and a voice declared that unto you, shall be given the mystery of the gospel. Instantly he was no longer in the left line walking toward the bottom right side of Jesus Throne.

Bill was near the bottom of some pyramid shaped type steps before Jesus Throne. Jesus was leaning forward watching him. Bill was preaching to two or three persons while backing up. He turned around and said to

Jesus, "what if I fall?" Jesus said, "I have two angels to bear you up to keep you from falling." When he looked around, two angels were behind him. Their wings were spread until they touched each other forming a net to catch him if he fell. He turned and began preaching again and almost instantly the two or three persons became a multitude climbing the stairs to walk before the throne of Jesus. This group was a multitude that passed before Jesus throne as he sat like a king in review. Not in a majestic fashion but leaning forward in a kindly, friendly, loving manner. Bill finally stood near the top of the stairs with a stretched out left arm as though directing them to walk before Jesus' Throne. This vision has always been before Bill. He considers this vision a personal commission and charge to be one of God's Deliverers and to set the captives free. He believes this freedom is physical, mental and spiritual. As the ministry of Jesus Christ is, so the ministry of Bill the deliverer should be.

The sun has risen on a majestic day.
A cloudless sky greets eagles, bees, and men.
Mankind rises; he flexes muscles, and brain.
A silent signal is given. Let my day's life begin.

An ordinary man, yet I carry the ability to succeed.
I am strong and have early in life set my goal.
For success, life has given me all that I need.
A voice crying freedom today must take its toll.

8. JUST AN ORDINARY FAMILY ** DESTINATION ** HOSTAGE

Bill and Marva left the church to the cheers and good wishes of a standing room only packed church. Bill was a fairly popular youth preacher and one of his affiliate youth persons had a marriage the same day. Her wedding was one hour before Bill's and only six blocks away. The results were two very large weddings. Bill and Marva could not believe the amount of presents they received. Marva's bedroom at her mother's house was filled to an overflow with presents. We wont have to buy some things for many years to come; stated Marva. This seemed an ideal beginning for what seemed like the marriage of the year for the young church couples.

The joys of marriage were wonderful. A smiling partner walking hand in hand in the shopping mall or sitting on the patio holding hands. Watching the television together and practicing the songs for the next service. For a while it seemed like a real life Cinderella story. But alas, Cinderella was only a dream. Soon real life set in. Every success story has a few hurdles that must be overcome and a few roadblocks that must be bypassed. Success is only noted at the end of the journey. A winner must first cross the finish line to receive the trophy. A crown is not worn at the beginning of the beauty pageant but at the end. Long live the king and queen of marriage.

The ministry was a whirlwind trip for the first two years. Bill accepted a church pastorate and Marva became a very dedicated pastor's wife. The church expanded rapidly and soon they were overseeing day care, a school from k thru 12, radio, TV, and a host of other church related activities.

Bill took things in stride but growth began to show a cry that sounded like I could use more help. Marva was doing an excellent job running the day care and decided to direct The Academy also. Marva's singing and TV appearances with Bill were terrific. Yet while all seemed like a perfect match outside, a horrible fire was burning that would make their children A Hostage Of The State.

As a teenager, Marva had lived a rather questionable life for about three years. Her mother had become frustrated with her life. Marva was sent off to dad to live. Dad was a rather flamboyant man about town so it was not surprising to see Marva adopt some of his characteristics. In those three years of freedom from sound parental authority, Marva managed to test drugs, alcohol, prostitution and a few other things. Bill was aware of some or her Pre-Christian escapades but did not count them as a jeopardy to their lives and ministry. All of us have sinned and come short of The Glory Of God. It was often pointed out that men of great stature as Moses, Paul, David, Jacob, Eli, Joshua, Samson, and Jonah had made some terrible errors during their faith walk but had ended in triumph.

Today as Marva and several of her women's group discussed plans for the upcoming midsummer conference, a different meeting was going on in the visiting room of the state prison. Troy was serving a twenty- five to life term. He was the father of Marva's oldest son, TJ. He had been one of her companions in the old sin life. He and Marva had separated and eventually his life caught up with him. He was serving a life sentence. Marva had changed her life and was now an on fire pastor's wife serving The Lord. Bill had adopted her son, TJ and life was rosy thus far.

I walked the way of the world so long,
My heart was sad and I began to cry.
It seemed that the yoke could not be broken.
I heard the voice of Jesus say, son let Me try.

My burdens lifted and I felt so free.
I changed my life to answer his call.
I am now presenting a brand new me.
Keep me Lord Jesus lest I again fall.

9. HELL'S GATES BEGINS TO MOVE

Troy's mother was upset a little more than usual as she visited Troy today. Troy's dad had just bought her a new house. They were just finishing up the final moving plans. Troy and his parents were now near the end of today's visit. "Troy we have made up our minds that we will not sell the house." "You are our only son and we have said we will keep it for you until you get out." "We have not given up hope that your appeals will work." "We believe that the three- strike law is one of the cruelest laws that was ever made in this state." "Why should you be put in jail for life for a simple street fight?" "Especially when so many people witnessed that he started the fight." "I think about that sometimes mom but it is too late to cry." "That was about a gang related incident that had happened over two years before then." "It was silly and I never should have gotten involved with them in the first place."

"I know son. We just can't roll back father time." "Son, your dad and I made a decision." "We are going to just leave the house vacant until you get out." "Well mom if you are going to do that, why don't you try to find Marva." "You know that my son should be big enough now." "Maybe you can let him stay in the house and keep it together for me." "I have been working on this appeal and if the appeal don't work I only have seven more years to go through here." "All right son. I will try to find them." "I heard that she got married." "I know that she moved out of state some time ago." "Your dad is retiring in three weeks." "We will take some time to travel and look for our grandson." "I sure hope he looks like you."
"You know Troy; this has been the hardest years of our life having you in this place; especially since you are our only son." "At least they let us

inside to sit and talk with you." "But honey when I had to talk to you on the other side of that glass, I went home and cried all night many times."

"You don't know how many times I felt like beating myself for not being more firm in disciplining you." "I still think if I had used more control on you, you would not be here." "Well, mom, you did what you thought was best." "I knew it was wrong to run with pot smokers, and pill poppers." "The nice car that the drug dealer had is what got my attention." "I didn't realize then that basically all of the dealers that I saw and worked with would all be jailed in less than a year." "When they came out of jail, many of them tried it again." "You know mom, over fifty- seven of my friends in that stuff have died violently that I know of." "You at least told me to stay away from them." "A whole lot more are probably dead." "If I was outside, there is no telling where I might be." "I might have been one of those pushing up daisies."

"In fact mom, do you know that I only know of one person that I believe was successful in using his ill gotten money." He was an eighteen-year-old boy that gave his money to his parents. They thought he was working on a job. He left the streets, went to school and became a regular law abiding person. His parents used the money he gave them to buy a house. He is the only dealer that I know of that did not use drugs and was only in the streets for a few months before coming to his senses. His parents still don't know his street history from what I understand at this time. "Mom it is too late to cry for me!" "Find my son and help me work on him to keep him out of a place like this."

A few weeks later Bill and Marva got a phone call. Her baby's grandparents were in town. They would like to see her and the child. Of course Marva and Bill were grateful that after several years they had not forgotten that they had a grandson. If only they could see the future. Behind the visit, a dark cloud was about to envelope their home. Their lives would never be the same. They were about to learn the reason the word said, evil communications corrupt good manners. They would know beyond a shadow of a doubt the meaning of the charge, come out from among them and be separated.

The meeting was great. They promised to visit the church the next time they were in town. They requested that their son be allowed to write his son. They said they had a house that they would give to Marva and TJ, the grandson if they ever came back to the state. Of course Bill was not excluded. They just did not know if he would be willing to accept their generosity. Bill and Marva were assured that if they came to that state before TJ became eighteen, the house would be theirs. After the age of eighteen, if TJ came to the state, the house would be his.

Two doors toward The Hostage Of The State were now open. A promise had been given. A lie had been planted. We will give you, (a house) had been heard. One, continual communication with a hostage that had been A Hostage Of The State for over ten years had now been opened. He was ten years trained as a hostage in (prison) doctrine. Two, a home of your own if you choose to leave your home sweet home. Was this just a sweet innocent offer of friendship and help? No! It was A Hostage Of The State Trap.

Troy's communication began as innocent letters to a son that he had not seen for several years. But Troy had one thing that most people do not have. That is time. Time to dream; time to let his mind wander. Time to learn prison art; time to write prison songs; time to remember the old life prior to prison years. Time to write and think about and suggest about how things can be, may be, will be, if only somehow we can cut loose the present ties of marriage, friends, family, and start over together. Marva and her family were about to learn that a man's ways don't change unless his spirit changes within him. Evil communications really do corrupt good manners. Friendship with the world or those outside of Christ, really is an enemy of Christ. The scriptures do not lie.

A persons companions speak well of him. The Hostage Of The State seeks a companion. Who will become one with me? A husband that is unfaithful in heart seeks a girlfriend. The wife that is unfaithful in heart seeks a boyfriend. The state system that has your child seeks ways to keep the children coming. "How can I be comforted unless I have enough children to pay my way?" Troy said, "I can't be free but if I can just have the joy of someone outside of this prison working with me." His parents said, "if only I can have someone helping my son. Surely he has changed. He needs somebody." The son said, "maybe the notes Troy slips inside for my mom with the instructions don't let Bill see them is all right." "Besides he sounds like a good dad."

It started out very small.
It was a small stream near a mountain top.
It stands now as a majestic waterfall
Cascading water with a two hundred foot drop.

Sin begins with a very innocent looking lie,
Most of us don't recognize it's tool.
It paints a picture of a friendly clown.
Beware friend, it is a king of sin desiring to rule.

10. THE HOSTAGE PATH IS COMPLETE.

The hostage path is now complete to Bill and Marva's house. It is a path of lying and deceit. It is a path of communication to transmit the same. A network that kills, steals, and destroys. A network that brings home violence, home dissension, home deceit, home lying, home disobedience, home distrust, home suspicion. A network that says the divorce court is waiting for the husband and wife. The girlfriend is waiting for the husband. The boyfriend is waiting for the wife. A network that says prison calls to the man. He will never hold a state or federal job again. He will never vote again. He will never be a fireman, policeman, or detective. The County Department Of Social Services waits for the children. They will become Hostages Of The State in another home. The adults will become Hostages Of The State in prison. A Hostage at the voting booth. A Hostage in the job market. Even your driver's license is subject to the Hostage Of The State policy and don't forget that your tax returns may be tapped also. Follow the pattern. Politics wont change it. The Prison System billions depends on The Hostages. The Social Services Welfare Budget Billions depends on The Hostage System. Every lawyer depends on The Hostage System. Now watch Marva as she embraces the system freely. Fortunately, God has already through the supernatural prepared Bill to set not only these captives but also the system captives free. It is bad today, but God's deliverer is on the way.

Marva was truly a very unsuspecting person when Troy first began writing his son TJ. The little give your mother my regards were so innocent sounding. Then the notes began coming. At first they were short poems or little sayings. Some were thankful for TJ's progress. Some were encouraging her to stay faithful to The Lord. Some were being grateful that she had found such a great husband.

Then the tempo changed. I get quite lonely here. Will you write me? I wish I could see you once more. Maybe you can take a vacation trip and visit me in my prison. Perhaps you could do some research to see if you could help my release. None of this information or practice was relayed to Bill. He was totally uninformed.

Without hardly trying, the trust bond between husband and wife was broken. The family walls had been breached. The family foundation of unity, harmony, sharing and peace was gone. A voice from prison was speaking freely in their home. The house now had two minds and a son, TJ in the middle; often times as a secret courier. God's original plan that these two (husband and wife) should be one had now been lost in this marriage. The one mind had now become two minds and the voice from prison had now created a third mind in the home. Disaster had arrived. Three minds could never become one.

One day when I felt most secure.
A little mosquito entered my house.
Because he was so very small.
I did not treat him like I would a mouse.

I made no effort to stop the bug.
I let him roam and then fly away.
But he left a gift within my home.
A virus disease that is here to stay.

11. DISMANTLING A FAMILY FROM WITHIN

Marva's life took on a new spirit. As Marva allowed herself to continually hear Troy's words and wishes, the spirit of rejection of God's Words was working full time. Marva began to slowly back off from the forefront of the women's ministry. Her constant church friends and close companions inside the congregation, soon became those with the least credible standards. Gradually she withdrew from every major leadership position in the church. Bill found himself speaking to Marva often in an attempt to inspire her to expand her ministry role instead of decreasing it. This proved to be of no avail. Bill's home had finally been penetrated by a spiritual enemy, an enemy that one could not see but knew that it was there.

Bill's love and compassion was tried to the utmost. He had originally been attracted to Marva because of her commitment to Christ. To see this dedication decrease pierced his heart daily. To watch The Anointing of God leave his wife broke his heart. His daily cry to God was, Lord keep me standing. I must stand or be lost. I want to stand, pure, holy, godly, never looking back, never turning around, or compromising. His prayer for Marva, was Lord restore her if possible. Never let Satan rejoice over taking her to hell. Lord restore today.

Little things began to happen that bothered Bill. Pieces of mail addressed to Marva that were sent to some of the weaker members address. Mail addressed to Marva going to a business that Marva frequented often. Bill soon found that being at the cousins did not always mean his wife was at the cousin's house. The drug store trip often meant I don't know where. Things got sorely worse. Alcohol, and cigarettes found in his wife's car. Meetings that ended at eight and a return home often after twelve. In renewing the conversation with Troy, TJ's prison held dad, Marva had also renewed contact with a crowd that still walked in that old life. Come out from among them and be separated had lost its meaning and effectiveness with Marva, the wife of the preacher. This same spirit now embraced TJ. The boy that was once considered on his way to becoming a great preacher and youth worker had now become associated with drugs, gangs, tobacco, and alcohol. Marva made it a point to maintain the influence of his dad, Troy, in both of their lives. Drugs and alcohol along with wayward girls and men soon became their life.

TJ became one of the most popular teens in the church prior to his open rebellion against God's Word. TJ appeared to be a born leader. Youth looked up to him. His peers honored and respected him enough to faithfully complete the spiritual assignments he would give them through the pastor's direction. He was looked up to and respected throughout his organization. TJ was expected to become a great spiritual leader.

In the wake of spiritual rebellion against God, This same popularity followed TJ outside of the church. Youth flocked around him. His charm was breath taking. His charisma was magnificent. It was just on the wrong side of the fence. TJ had began working not for Christ but against Christ in his daily life activities.

Bill's home now had the mark of Eli and his Devil Worshiping or Baal Worshiping sons. The book of First Samuel was now alive in the preacher's house. A backsliding mother and a backsliding son were visible before God's People. How many people would perish and die spiritually over the fall of these two? The Devil now had a strong foothold in the preacher's house. The enemy was no longer outside the home but inside it. Bill's table now had two betrayers that came to dinner daily. Unfortunately they were family members. This was a bitter pill to swallow and one of the most severe tests of a man's love that can arrive in this life. The preacher had vowed to stand in spite of all tests. Would he stand this family test? If Job stood, so can Bill.

TJ formed his own gang. Marva was TJ's private mentor. Robbery, and robbery with assault, car theft, drug sales, drug use and several other charges began to pile up against TJ. Bill was unaware of any of these charges because TJ was using another name. With Marva's help, TJ had obtained documentation and actually had two separate identities. Bill was quite devastated when he accidentally found this out while checking at TJ's high school office. Can you imagine a teenage son using an alias and engaging in criminal activities with the help and assistance of a mother? Troy, from   inside prison, (A Hostage Of The State) had reached outside prison into a preacher's home (Bill) and managed to corrupt both his wife and son.

Both TJ and Marva had laid the church on the side almost totally. Bill found himself fighting the charge from his own family that he was too religious for them to stay with him. Bill found himself being often challenged about his doctrine, discipline, and teaching on every hand. Bill had built his lifetime foundation on faith in God's Holy Word. Now an effort was being made almost on a daily basis to chip away at his faith, hope, ambition, and love.

Many nights while others slept Bill found himself walking through his house and his church crying out to The Lord. Lord I believe, help my unbelief and give me strength to stand faithful to you became a daily prayer. He knew he was being tried. He knew his life for eternity was on the line. He knew he had to win. He knew The Lord would be with him always even to the ends of the earth. He also knew that it was his choice whether or not to stand. He knew he had to make it.

One of Bill's greatest fears was the knowledge that he was an example to so many people. He knew that if he failed, many weak Christians might use his failure as an excuse to walk in sin. The words of the epistles that we should judge that none of us should put a stumbling block in our brother's way was a prime principle in Bill's doctrine. He knew that his example was critical to some people's salvation. Someone other than himself would live or die because of him.

To Bill this was devastating. Yet in the midst of this, his greatest spiritual battle, he found that to his amazement he had a peace and joy within himself that he never dreamed possible. His spiritual works never ceased. Bill's personal peace did not stop membership loss. He did lose most of his members. Some left because of his son's activities. Some left because of his wife's activities. Bill never discussed his wife or their problems with anyone outside of his immediate family which was his wife and his children. Many that heard rumors could not believe that his wife and not Bill was the guilty one in the divorce and separation. Bill himself did not get the divorce. He felt that he would be in violation of God's Law if he did not fail to do all that he could to maintain the marriage and to restore it after the divorce was granted.

Bill still feels that legal bible divorce is only permitted when a spouse engages in sex with a third party. God said these two should be one, not three or more become one. Bill still holds to the fact that God judges every act of adultery. He believes that God is fair and holds that Hebrews 13;4 will not let either party get by whether it be the husband, wife, boyfriend, or girlfriend. This includes lustful thinking. Bill declares that the first road to physical adultery is mental thinking adultery. Even though Bill could not pinpoint where he had been wrong in the divorce, he still felt that he could have done more to save the marriage. He did feel that he was right in not leaving until Marva evicted him in favor of her boyfriend.

I Corinthians; ch.7 was Bill's guide in this area. He believed that if Marva was pleased to live with him, he should not put her away. He knew that if he left, he would be out of God's Will. He felt that we inside the church were often guilty of spiritual adultery toward our spiritual husband, Jesus Christ. Jesus did not put us away every time we committed sin and served Satan. Every sin that we commit is an act of spiritual adultery was a part of Bill's teaching. Jesus' mercy and grace gave us a chance to be forgiven and return to his love. The 15 and 16 verses were referred to often. If Marva leaves, I must let her. If she repents and changes back to Jesus Christ then I have had a part in her restoration. The day that Marva evicted him in favor of her boyfriend was like a sunset to face a moonless night according to Bill's description. Only The Lord Jesus could give him the light and encouragement to stay saved at that time. ** But He did. ** Hallelujah** Bill! ** shout!

The worst fears of marriage are now staring at a husband and wife. The dream of children in college, doctors, executives, chef cooks, ballerinas, and movie stars is gone. The retirement fund and life of travel is gone. The vacation cottage has disappeared and the present house is in danger of being lost. The Cinderella dream is lost and the dark cloud of fear, uncertainty, despair, regret, anxiety, and if I had only done this is now the chief thought occupation.

So many times I have heard the words
If I could have known before it was too late.
But God always spoke in that still small voice.
It was easy to say sorry Lord, that's not my fate.

I know I will answer for the trouble I caused.
I know I can find no excuse.
Did I train my family to be the best they could,
Without hatred, anger, malice, or abuse?

They were only with me a few short days.
Could I train them for a lifetime and eternity?
No not by myself. Then I heard the Master's voice.
Send them to me. I have the key. I will set them free.

12. JUSTICE SYSTEM *** RIPE FOR HOSTAGES

Every great nation must have a system of checks and balances for the government. What happens when an enforcement official declares that the law does not mean what it says? What happens when justice depends upon which judge you stand before? Liars will beget liars and thieves will beget thieves. When justice in a nation depends upon which judge you stand before, failure has already began. The question is only how long it will take to become complete chaos in the land? Bill and Marva lived in a typical American big city; one of the ten largest cities in America. The city itself had one of the best crime rates in the country. Yet listen to the actual partial record of Bill's block while he resided there.

Lonnie had just finished working on his new car. He bought it used and was attempting to get all the bugs out. He was now going to drive it around the block and drove off with a few curious neighbors standing by cheering him on with a good natured ribbing. As Lonnie drove off in his cherry red T-Bird. A policeman approaching from the opposite direction, saw him as he pulled out of his driveway and made a u turn. As Lonnie made his second right turn in his trip around the block the policeman stopped him.

Lonnie stated that he had broken no laws and lived on the next street at the driveway the policeman had seen him exit from. He asked the policeman why he had stopped him. The policeman stated that he was a gang banger and pointed to his tattoos as evidence. Lonnie explained that his three tattoos were for his cousin that had died and a cross was in the middle with his cousin's name. The other two were explained as his mother and dad's first names. A backup person arrived and advised the stopping officer that Lonnie had no record or history of crime. He also verified Lonnies' address. The backup officer was told, "you are here for back up!" "Don't tell me how to do my job." Lonnie was handled roughly and taken to the station. About four hours later Lonnie was released after another officer at the station confronted the arresting officer.

How can you be taken to a police station in handcuffs with no actual crime having been committed and after being advised that the person has no criminal record or history? This is very scary. It reminds me (a junior historian) of the Gestapo days when Hitler was rising to power. Police or any other authority must never be misused in a free society. A whole neighborhood was affected by one officer's arrogance. Imagine how easily a nation can be affected by one man in authority in error.

The question in the block was why should an officer of the law be so anxious to claim a person for jail time? Why was a young man leaving his driveway so rudely confronted by a policeman for no apparent reason? Why was a backup officer's information totally ignored? Why did it take another street officer and not the officer's superiors to correct the situation? This looked like Hostage Recruitment.

Jake was driving when he was struck by a hit and run driver. A passing motorist witnessed the accident and stopped. Jake left his wife and child with the two witnesses and pursued the driver. He caught up to him in a downtown area and hailed a police car. He advised the police that this man had hit his car. He had pursued him and was now turning him over to them. He told him that his wife and child along with two witnesses were waiting for him at the accident scene. To his surprise the driver told the officer that he was driving along when Jake and some more men began chasing him.

Jake was immediately held by the police and manhandled. Jake begged them to at least go back to where he said the accident happened and check with the two waiting witnesses and his wife and child. After much hassle they finally did do that. To the neighbor, this looked like a forget the facts and take a jail hostage episode. After observing the scene the officers advised Jake that the two of them Jake and the hit and run driver could hammer it out with the insurance company. No tickets issued, no report filed. Only a reporter of an accident slightly roughed up and a perpetrator freed.

<u>When an enforcer of the law becomes the breaker of the law on a regular basis, truth hides and injustice, lies, bribery and favoritism, rule the streets.</u> We have seen pockets of this atmosphere. We cannot allow it to continue unless we are fans of self-destruction of this free nation. Liberty means freedom for all, the foundation of our nation. The badge or the political bar should mean that I am your defense. A protector of the poor, a unifier of families.

The neighbors watched as the boyfriend of a neighbor kicked the door in. He was a convicted felon and drug dealer. Several children inside ran out terrified. Some concerned neighbors called the police. The police did arrive. What did the police do? Talked to the man and let him go.

Several drug users went back inside the house. Two of those returning inside were felons convicted of car theft and robbery. One was associated with a gang, was on probation and had been convicted of assault and robbery. Those minors that had just witnessed the violence also returned inside the house. A court order was on file that those minors should not witness violence within that home.

Within a couple of weeks the minors were Hostages Of The State. The drug dealing boyfriend and the drug using mother were free. The robbers, felons, gang members, and parolees were still free residents of the house. Where was the father? Barred from the house and barred from the children. Upon what grounds? His complaints were designed to paint an unfair picture of the mother, said his wife's Social Worker. He never had a criminal record. His driving record was clean, his government job carried a security level clearance and per investigation, his life was basically spotless. Why was the deck stacked against him? The mother and boy friend had a friend inside The Social Service Office. A friendly word goes a long way for a friend when you are among friends.

What about the children? They became Hostages Of The State when a father could or should have been caring for them. Why were the facts ignored and the father not allowed to challenge them? This is one reason

55

that I personally advocate that The Social Workers be subjected to a lie detector test when a parent request it. When an agency is more ready to incarcerate a person than to return one to their home, it is prison mentality. This explains to me why there is a periodic upsurge in building prisons. At times more prisons than schools are built in some states.

A part of Bill's early life was spent in a Pennsylvania village called Liberty. The area was populated by many immigrants from Poland and Yugoslavia. One of the history teacher's favorite teaching slogans was America give me your poor, your weak, your hopeless. America's liberty, freedom for the poor, weak, and hopeless was somehow etched in his mind as this is what is supposed to be in this free land of America. Now, while facing reality, even Bill's childhood education is becoming clouded thinking.

It is a joy to have you as my friend.
We have meant much for years to each other.
We have often held each other's hand.
At times we have been closer than a brother.

I thank you for bailing me out of trouble.
I know that at times I was really wrong.
My conscience often gives me a terrible struggle.
Sometimes it is hard to sing a victory song.

If I could only always somehow do right.
You would not have to protect me with a lie.
Can I possibly be made over or start again?
Simply ask truth and justice, they say just try.

13. DREAM CASTLE BUST

A family begins with two. One husband, one wife. What is the plan? One rooster, one chicken, one buck, one doe, one lion, one lioness, two birds, one male, one female. What is the goal? Little ones raised, taught, trained, and instructed by the parents until they are able to step out on their own and continue the pattern of life. Lions do not train birds, nor does chickens train deer. <u>There is no substitute for parental training.</u> One parent forsaking a nest or family can wreak havoc on future generations of the family. Only a parent is capable of having total love and concern for his family. One erring parent can activate a whole passel of waiting Hostage Takers. Beware parent. The prisons, jails, foster homes, adoption persons, family care persons, family lawyers, and family courts are waiting on you oh foolish parent. Listen to the story of Marva and Bill. Their dream has exploded and their castle has burst. Only the dismantling remains.

Bill arrives at the credit union to deposit his weekly savings in each of his children's savings account. Each child is allowed to spend from his weekly portion and the one that saves the most gets a bonus for the week. Today when Bill prepares to deposit the weekly allowance, he is quite surprised to find that each account has been emptied. In his mind, he quietly exclaims, TJ and Marva. He utters a silent prayer. Lord I hope I am wrong, if I am right, please bring quick repentance for this was the children's savings. How will I be able to replace it? Thank you for direction.

This was only the beginning. Bill always expected a sizable income tax return and this year was no different. The tax return was great. The surprise was the over ten thousand dollar bill that showed up at the same time. It seemed that the heavens opened and decided to rain down problems. Unknown bills began to show up at Bill's house. Tickets on the automobiles that no one could explain. Some of these were from cities that every house driver denied being in. Checks that disappeared from the mail and ended up being cashed by unknown persons. The phone rang continually from bill collectors looking for unknown persons at his home phone number. His home mailbox began receiving mail for various unknown persons. All of the children's grades took a dive and two were failing. The news that his son was cursing at school brought Bill to his knees in a lengthy fast. Still the problems persisted. Neither TJ nor Marva made a change and all the children seemed to follow their lead.

It seemed that Bill was on one side and all the family on the other side. Bill was basically by himself in his own family. To further complicate matters, Bill's congregation was now less than a handful. He found himself spending his nights in prayer as sleep fled and ten p.m. to four a.m. became the homecoming time for TJ and Marva. To make matters worse, Marva often would pick the children up from school and bring them home when she arrived. Imagine your child arriving home at one to two a. m. and later. Bill's life was a literal nightmare.

Marva's family had at one time almost all belonged to Bill and Marva's ministry. None of Marva's family at that time could believe that she had become so terribly backslidden. They often became ignorant supporters of her wrong by providing baby sitting or weekend or overnight visits for the children. Bill was reluctant to reveal the extent of his wife's actions for fear of destroying her reputation. He had long ago found that some of the company business trips were not company trips. Some of the incentive trips to vacation spots were not paid for by the company. Still, Bill found himself seeking the Lord daily in hopes that all this would change.

Bill reminded himself almost daily that the church of Jesus Christ was met by Jesus daily intercession to His Father God for its repentance and perfection. If Paul did turn to the Lord after being the number one church persecutor of his day, so can Marva. If John Mark could become valuable to God and a helper to The Apostles after becoming a quitter, then so can Marva. Bill thought often of Peter. This disciple was rebuked harsher than any other disciple and yet heard the charge to feed God's Sheep. His personal commitment to himself was, as long as Marva is in the home, I shall pray and hope that she turn again to Christ Jesus. If she ever leaves the home, I shall pray continually that God's Mercy restore her again.

Is there hope in the eyes of The Lord Jesus? Bill considered the fact that the scripture said we shall be like gold tried in the fire seven times. Yet when we come out of the fire we are like pure gold. Bill chose to consider this session of his life as God's Training Ground. He felt that this was his fire but if he stood, he would be like pure gold in Christ Jesus sight. Can he make it? Will Marva make it? Only Christ Jesus knows of a surety. Bill knew he could make it.

Bill knew that his family was being torn apart and he seemed helpless to stop it. His tears and stress was now almost unbearable. Still, he had to stand. He was a light, an example, a husband and a father under pressure. His stomach was upset daily. His mind fought him for stability. His hair became streaked with gray. His conscience questioned him daily.

He knew the scripture that a man that did not provide for his house was worse than an infidel. Bill felt strongly that if he could not control his own house, he should not be in charge of God's House or the church. He worried that he was not seen in his house as a perfect leader. Jesus was his example. He comforted himself with the fact that Jesus' Church was still disobedient at times. He knew that confession and repentance to Christ Jesus worked. Still, Bill fought doubt and fear daily. Should he continue in the ministry? was a major question! This was not like a job. This was an assignment, a choice, a commitment, a career, and an ambition that would affect many lives for possibly many generations in the future. His family had to stand if possible.

Neither the wife, the society, the government nor any other person could make the call to save his family and future. It had to be Bill on the front line. God had established that the husband should be the priest king of the family. It was Bill's responsibility to turn the family around if it was possible. Even though it was his God Given Duty, the only person that he could truly insure receiving salvation was his own. The challenge was his. Others had stood. So would Bill. If no one else, Bill shall overcome today. Bill will fight one day at a time. Bill rebuked himself often for not being a better defense against his troubles. Yet in those times he turned to the

Lord Jesus' session with the disciples after his resurrection. He rebuked them for their unbelief. Then he commanded them to go into all the world and preach the gospel to every creature. Bill said, I have been rebuked by both life and myself. I must humble myself and preach sound gospel until I die. I must stand that Jesus shall not rebuke me in the final judgment day. I must and I shall live without obvious sin or willful disobedience to God's Word daily.

Today I rejoice that I am still alive
At times in the past, I often wished I wasn't born.
Sorrows seemed to cloud my joy and stir my fear.
Then the clouds moved back as I sounded my horn.

Amazing things happened when I began to speak.
When I chose right and made my stand.
Some things I thought would never change.
They are now reformed throughout the land.

Joy often fled and tried to run away.
But God's word held me in its grip.
Joy from the well of salvation had to stay.
The lord held my hand. I could not slip.

At times the sun seemed about to set
But somehow the light kept on shining.
Be still my son I am not finished with you yet,
Seemed words on which I found myself dining.

14. HIDE THE CHILDREN *** HOSTAGE TAKERS ARE HERE

Bill now likens himself in part to The Patriarch Job. His very principles of life are being challenged. Bill had been working with the anti-drug agents for some   time. At least five narcotic agents had been saved in his church. Their stories and testimonies of the destructive effect of drugs had helped consolidate Bill's conviction. Bill believed and taught that every drug dealer is a serial killer and should be handled as such. Every drug user is a supporter of a mafia or drug cartel type criminal. They support death, broken homes and families and are one of the largest threats to Family Stability in America.

Bill laments, I am like Job. Job said, "The thing that I feared is come upon me." The wife is divorced and a drug user. How did it happen? Her boyfriend is a drug dealer. How did it happen? Alcoholics and drug users frequent the house that my children live in. How did it happen? My children are failing in school. How did it happen? The older children have been encouraged to become juveniles. How did it happen?

Bill remembered one of his favorite persuasions to encourage Afro-Americans to stop drug use in their society. He would point out that theirs was the only neighborhoods in America that were allowed to sell drugs openly in the streets. He would point out that this was a payback for Martin Luther King's Civil Rights Leadership that was partly successful to promote Equality For Blacks in America. This drug practice promotes black genocide. He remembered his discussions about how crack was released within the black community. He liked to point out that our government had knowledge of this plan for at least five years prior to the drug crack being released within the ghettos and appeared to do nothing to hinder the plan. In some areas Government Action appeared to support this criminal backed plan.

As Bill allowed himself to reflect in one of his weaker or more troubled moments, he literally shuddered at some of his own warnings that were ignored. Bill was especially concerned about some of the anti drug persons that were being targeted to silence their voices. Bill considered this effort an informational blackmail effort. One major lawyer in an Eastern city was a personal friend of Bill's. He was very active in anti-gang and anti-drug campaigning. His son soon found himself surrounded by several new friends. Both young men and young ladies. In a short while, his son found himself involved in some of their deeds. What had happened?" His son was targeted and lured into anti society activity by organized crime in hopes of stopping the lawyer's campaign. Did it work?" Not in that case. The lawyer stood in spite of the son's failure to remain removed from dishonesty. There was some loss of influence and effectiveness but this lawyer maintained his position. He still considered himself a success in a moral fight that he believed in.

Bill remembered the day several drug lords visited his church on a Sunday morning. They came driving their Cadillacs and wearing their gold chains. They visited with many of the congregation after morning worship. One of their main goals was to find out if Bill was truly motivated to stop drugs in the community for the Afro-Americans sake or was he just a snitch for the local police. They went away with the idea that at least what Bill was doing was deep rooted in Bill's heart and had been there from his youth. Both alcohol and drugs were considered by Bill as a destroyer of the poor.

As Bill allowed himself to reflect further, darts of pain and fear with uncertainty pierced his heart. Was the boyfriend of his ex wife the same drug dealer he had witnessed to over five years ago as he sat in a car in East Palo Alto counting drug sale money? Had his wife and son became one of the targets of the drug boys to silence a preacher who had vowed from his youth to fight to free families from the scourge of alcohol and drugs as well as willful acts of sin against the Eternal God? Were they a target because Bill had dedicated himself to a minimum of ten hours a week to convert or change the street vendors of drug inspired violence and death? Bill will probably never know. He has vowed since that day of mental heartbreak that he will never allow such a thought to remain in his mind for a minute. Such thoughts may knock on the door, said Bill, but I will never let them in again.

Why not Bill? The Hostage Takers do not care how you or your children get into their hands. Their salary depends on your incarceration. The nice names are Custody, Treatment Plan, Foster Care, Out Of Home Placement, Half Way House, Drug Therapy, Out Patient, and a multitude of other names. The truth is not to give me your tired, your weary, your needy, your poor. My teacher spoke these words about men and women that came to America to prosper and most did. We as a people have become knit into the world's greatest earthly nation. This saying spoke of a time when qualified parents taught their own children to excel or just do the best you can with a mother and a father as their partner and chief trainer. This was and still is the best formula for success. This should still be a time when a man or woman should seek their ambitions and careers with all the immediate family help possible and without the danger of you or your children becoming Hostages Of The State.

Local, State and Federal Government represents the strength of our nation. Ask John Adams. According to history he was probably the most persuasive of the signers of the Constitution of The United States Of America. I believe we all know the story of the rag tag army that George Washington used to defeat the greatest nation in the world at that time. Our rag tag army begins with one. That is either you or I. Our greatest beginning was not standing by and allowing the government to control us. Greatness was achieved by the people becoming what was needed in the government to achieve honesty, justice, honor, fairness and the strength to impart the same to those that rule and govern our nation. This should not be a time when government authorized people look over your shoulder and decide whether or not you raised your children as they thought. If a criminal intent is there, we should rejoice in comfort, knowing that Uncle Sam is there for us as a policeman against evil.

The Hostage Taker does not consider America's diversity. It was diversity that made our nation great. Why must diversity be destroyed by a Hostage Taker? No American should allow themselves to submit to a system that destroys Family Values. Who will teach your children morals? Who will teach your children religion? Who will seek to set the lifetime goal of your child? No one else has the love, care, conviction, and concern of a parent. God made this so. Only fools will give this joyous privilege to another.

No American should surrender this freedom without a great boxing ring performance. Will you fight for your family freedom or surrender to an agency? Bill is pushing a grocery cart inside the produce market of his neighborhood grocery store as he meditates on these thoughts. I will fight! yells Bill unconsciously. He looks around at a few startled people inside the market place. He shrugs his shoulders and continues shopping. He repeats to himself silently over and over. I will fight for my family. I must fight for my family. If I don't fight who will arise as defenders of the family? I can do it. I am well able. I am qualified or The Lord would not have allowed this task to come. I am and I shall be more than a conqueror for my family. Little did Bill know that he was about to take on The County, The State, Congress, and the Constitutional Standard itself in his efforts to reclaim his children from A Hostage Of The State Situation. His vow today would be tried beyond measure in this America. He, the moralist father has been evicted from the home. His children have been put on a downhill treadmill with a label reading destination ** Hostage Of The State** separated from a moral standard, a home filled with drugs and alcohol and a live in drug dealer, a drug using mother along with a house with several felony inhabitants ** formula ** hostage.

I awoke this morning to find a terrible thing.
My child's bed is empty. Is this a dream?
Some confusion existed in the ex spouse house,
But that was common, or so it seemed.

I can't imagine my separated spouse,
Being unworthy to raise my child.
After all they helped raise nine,
With a lot of tears but a few more smiles.

They frowned when speaking to the child.
They grabbed the child by the arm.
They loudly said, get in the car!

Throwing snowballs may cause great harm.

Now childless Gretchen heard those words.
She called 911 and yelled child abuse.
The hostage takers came. Their remedy**
Your children can no longer be loose.

As A Hostage Of The State, I train them now.
They rise, dress, eat and sleep at my command.
Ideas, methods, manner, shall be shaped by me.
If returned, a different child will walk the land.

15. HELPLESS ***** OR ***** SYSTEM FAILURE

Marva had filed for divorce some time before and because of the no fault divorce law recognized by most states, it was a foregone conclusion. Divorce would be granted. Bill did not contest the divorce but did file a petition with the court for custody of his children. The judge was exceptionally understanding and actually took one hour in personal counsel with Bill and Marva seeking to restore the marriage and prevent divorce. His main issue was the children. It did not work. Marva still demanded a divorce, demanded the house be sold and proceeds be divided between her and Bill. Marva also demanded child custody. All of these were granted.

The divorce proceedings was a great eye opener for Bill. He had always sought to maintain a presentable home that would make a Christian proud. No alcohol, profanity, drugs or tobacco in the home and three days a week attending church service. To his surprise Bill found himself being labeled a religious abuser. To insist that minor children attend service that often, was cruel?

Bill considered mandatory five day a week school training of his children under non-believers and atheists a major insult to his faith. He was shocked to find himself being the accused inside the courts. Church three times a week, four and a half hours a week to learn moral values as given by The Creator Himself and later demonstrated by the world's most perfect man! Now to be called an abuser to teach against violence, deceit and immorality and trying to instill a decent life example of fairness, honesty, justice, love and equity in my children! What has America stooped to? cries Bill! Are we so degenerate that we demand a child's corruption? If this is so, then every devil worshipper and every person believing in killing children for human sacrifice is as justified as our court system. Why? Because we have reversed the meaning of lies and truth, of love and hatred, of honesty and crime, of fairness and justice with corruption and anarchy.

Bill was extremely surprised to find so much hostility within the counselors and lawyers at the idea that his wife be given a drug test. He was advised by a court counselor and two social workers that the children are not removed from a mother's care because of drugs. Bill was advised that if a mother went through the court offered program she would be allowed to retain custody of her children. This idea mentally infuriated Bill since he had taught for years that whenever drugs are involved in a parent, the children should be legally removed. Bill was very emphatically reminded that this is not the case in this city.

Bill was truly surprised to hear the supervisor of the child complaint dept interrupt one of her counselors as she talked to him. Her message to Bill was to cease and desist from calling in any complaint against Marva. She felt that Bill was inventing the issues to discredit Marva for the sake of him receiving child custody. Bill assured her that he was only working on behalf of the children's safety when they report it to him. Bill still ponders the reason for this outburst. The supervisor was aware that the boyfriend was a convicted drug dealer living in the home. He was still on probation along with three other persons at that time living in the same home with Bill's children. Their charges included, car theft, robbery, assault and drug possession.

In spite of all of Bill's dissatisfaction with the court, the top of the list came when a court appointed counselor was speaking to Bill. His statement to Bill was this. Bill you are only a husband. Your complaints mean nothing. All Marva has to say is that you are lying. It is her word against yours. You will always lose.

Bill found out that if he learned nothing else, he learned how old fashioned he was to believe as the scripture has said. One couple was under a court order to attempt reconciliation. The major debate in court today was whether or not the wife could take her children with her when she went out of town to spend the weekend with her significant other. He was on a weekend release from prison. Her legal husband was objecting to the children accompanying her on these visits.

Another debate was whether the spouse could question the other party when their significant other came to the house to pick them up. The judge explained that they could not even inquire where they were going, what time they would return, nothing at all. He said that they were adults with full control over their lives and desires. The legal spouse could not interfere.

Bill had a truly hard time listening to some of the courtroom cases. He thought; what happened to husbands love your wife and wife love your husband ***(not the significant other)? He wondered if they knew the meaning of submit your selves one to another as a husband and wife. He had no problem explaining to himself why the divorce rate was well over fifty percent in some areas in America and why over half of the children in America are raised with one parent. Knowing that over eighty percent of crimes in America are committed by persons from a single parent home weighed heavily on Bill. He now found himself in that dangerous number. Will we ever learn the meaning of these two shall be one in marriage?

Guilt and self- condemnation became Bill's greatest accusers during these court proceedings. He felt totally helpless. His court voice was completely stopped. Not one of his desires for the family was granted. He often wandered how the first judge can be so right in his counsel and assessments and the final recommendations by the family counselors be so wrong. Bill found that his religious standard that he so highly prized was now his chief enemy as far as the court was concerned. <u>Drugs, alcohol, truancy, violence, armed robbery, car theft, all won over a religious standard that taught a clean home both spiritually and naturally.</u> Was this a rare case or was this an isolated system failure?

Where did you get that idea? Those were some of the crimes that the people in the house that the children were living in at the time of the divorce were guilty of. How did Bill know? His friend had an attorney request the records and submitted them on behalf of Bill during the proceedings. Did it help? No. <u>No wonder America , at the time of writing</u>

this chapter, has over two million two hundred thousand Hostages in major prisons and several million more Hostages in Halfway Houses, Foster Care, Out Of Home Placement, Child Care, Rehab Programs, Recovery Houses, etc. Many of these are innocent children.

Only two people were in the land.
Daily they walked and talked with their creator.
They could not imagine the evil they would cause,
By disobeying The Lord a few days later.

It seemed so easy to yield to their whims.
After all they had desires of their own.
They were the parents of all men and women.
Surely God would never leave them alone.

When God placed Adam and Eve in the garden,
He gave them both a condition.
The blessings of The Lord are forever more.
But only to those who hear God and listen.

Today we have lost so much of God's word.
We have forgotten the promises that are ours.
Too many of us sheep have gone blind.
We can't see that most shepherds are liars.

16. NO BRAKES

The final divorce decree called for a day of celebration for Marva and her friends. To them, this was freedom being granted. Bill's children were able to spend the week with him. Little did they know that this was the beginning of the darkest days of their life. Drugs, alcohol, violence, deceit, sexual abuse, thefts, all became their constant companions. Any mention by the children of home activities that Bill disagreed with found the speaker being disciplined by Marva or her household when they returned home.

Bill himself was not allowed near the house per court order. Still almost every day calls came in to Bill with a history of activities in the vicinity of his old residence. Bill was still looked up to by many as one of God's true preachers but even Bill himself found many moments to doubt his standing with God. He often prayed, Lord I don't see it, but there must be something here. What is it if it is here? I feel so unworthy. Where is my sin? Where is my fault?

The judge had insisted that the children have visitation with Bill on the weekends. This was always looked forward to by Bill. Still there was always an aftermath. Almost every Sunday a complaint was lodged with The Children Service that the sermons were against Marva. Bill expected that every Monday he would get a call requesting a sermon change. Every week Bill's answer was the same. God decides the sermon. I just preach it.

With the divorce over and the buyout of the property complete the family division was finalized. Marva and the children moved to another city and the ride to Hostage City began. Bill made himself available for every emergency that arose. He found himself as he put it a long distance pick up and return baby sitter. Needless to say, the clock was ticking. A mother and drugs is only a time bomb. Complicate the room with a drug dealer and a fire is imminent. Place two more drug users in the room and it is two seconds before an explosion. Add a teenage gang member and the volcano has erupted. The hot lava has begun to flow.

Marva's move proved to be a living disaster. Her family that had always extended their hand now turned their back on her. None of them had known the extent of her erring ways. They had all felt that Bill was the culprit and always held out the hand of help to her and the children. Now Marva had to go it alone. The children received some help and guidance from the relatives but basically the children had to become self- sufficient or raise themselves most of the time. The Hostage Takers has now been alerted. They are on the way. They can't be stopped. There is no brakes on drugs. It takes your food, your health, your sound mind of reason, your money, your job, your children, your freedom, and finally, your life. The Hostage Takers have arrived. Where are your children Bill? I come to claim them.

The hostage said you were an unfit mother.
And you sir, were reported as an unfit dad.
I have not read the full report yet,
But for your family, that is very bad.

You now have a record as long as you live.
It will read that you neglected your child.
Can you look in a mirror, read a true accusation,
And walk away with a truly innocent smile?

Guilt and shame will always hide within.
It buries itself inside a corner of your heart.
If you don't find the savior's redemption.
You will never be eternal, only a temporary part.

Marva's divorce settlement money is soon gone. Her drug-dealing boyfriend has bailed out of a sinking ship. The down payment on the house has expired and the house is lost. Charges of drug possession and driving under the influence are now hounding the family. What do you do? Head for Colorado with another drug dealer who is also a snitch. The end of the line is here. The Hostage Takers are waiting.

17. THEY HAVE MY CHILDREN

THE DOCUMENTARY BEGINS **** your child is now a state hostage ****the child is a juvenile prisoner **   truth now becomes shocking
You are now entering a child's world. Not a world of goblins, witches, scarecrows, tin men and talking trees.
This is a world of State or Agency Control this is a legal world of speculation, lies, and unchallenged authority. Legal Dictators that scoff at the written law and laugh in the face of parents. They mock lawyers and ignore every other legal authority. This is the Ultimate Child Prison.
This is Human Resource *** Social Service *** Foster Care a world without Parental Authority
This is my documentary

Nine A.M. In the morning, the phone rings. Mr. **** yes this is him speaking. This is Colorado Social Services. We have your children in custody in our state. You do? Yes. We picked them up from the mother's residence two days ago. We picked up two of the children from school on the same day. Give me the address and I will be there as soon as I can. The drive will take about twenty hours. Verify the address to pick them up. I am on my way as soon as I get dressed. That wont be necessary Mr. *** It will take us a couple of days to process the paperwork and after that we will contact you and put them on a plane for the return. You mean I don't have to do anything but wait for a couple of days? That's right. Do you have a phone number for me to call? This is the number for you to contact the person that will actually be handling the children's case.

The initial Social Welfare contact seemed to go quite well. I was assured that as soon as the preliminaries were over, I would be contacted and my children put on a plane and sent home. After about three weeks of a different excuse every week, I decided to check with a lawyer. Two local state lawyers assured me that the procedure stated was the proper one and the children should be on the way to being returned because the law was the same across the country. This sounded encouraging but when I called the agency to verify this new item of home study arose. From the time that this item arose until six months later a new allegation, complaint, or stated suspicion arose against me as set forth by the Colorado Human Resource Services almost weekly. The original time line of I will send them on a plane in a few days kept being expanded until it became well over a year and still no concrete deadline in sight.

I checked with several lawyers in several states to verify the law. The law is the same throughout the country. I checked with six Colorado lawyers and six Colorado Civil Rights Lawyers. To my surprise, all agreed that the law was the same. But strangely enough most of them had reservations about Jefferson County and Their System In Place.

I was advised that first, their system was set up for maximum retention. Second, the parent that would receive the children would be accused, vilified, or in any way found unworthy to receive their children back in their home. Third, I was told that they could or would post pone things indefinitely by using six- month increments to make decisions. This sounded very illegal but it came from so many in one state I hoped it would not be true.

My main question was how could such a practice be so wide spread and not be challenged? The answer! Get one crooked judge that can do anything without being challenged and you have a breach in the American System that may never be corrected. The second answer was what parent with money has their children in the system? Who has money to challenge them? I don't have money but I vowed to challenge this system. This rag tag preacher has a rag tag army of poor parents. We are the George Washington army that wins over the king.

In order to be accurate in my information, I checked with over twenty lawyers and four court systems outside of Colorado in several states. Most of the legal information supporting my Civil Rights Suit came from the ALR reports of The San Jose Law Library. The Colorado Code For Human Resources is the foundation of my original question and charges against The Colorado Human Resource Service of Jefferson County Colorado. This with the Civil Rights Declaration Of Congress .

Much detailed information of my documentary is taken from the volume of Child Welfare Services and The Children's Code used by Jefferson County Colorado. <u>The Constitution Of The United States Of America and several cases already fought and won is actually the foundation of The Family Civil Rights Suit to stop the wholesale incarceration of our children.</u> After settling on my charges and The Civil Rights Suit against the Jefferson County Colorado Agency, I did check with lawyers in several other states simply to verify information.

<u>Strictly in jest, I call these charges the Isaac Charge. Why? Because the head of The Service in Jefferson County at the time laughed at me. He said,(I know what the law says but it is debatable). You don't agree. Get a lawyer. Isaac means laughter.</u>

THESE ARE MY ORIGINAL CHARGES

<u>Charge</u> ** (a) unlawful retention of the fore named children.
Human Service Code * 26-5.3-102 (c), (d) * 26-5-3-104 (2), 26-5.3-106 (1.5) * 26-5.3-106 (2)b * 26-5.5-102 (f) * (g), 26-5.5-104 (2a,3b) ** specifically stated is failure to implement first priority to reunite my children with me their father.
<u>Charge</u> ** (b) Human Service Code * 26-5.3-102 (d) *26-5.3-104 (1),(2) * 26-5.3-105 (1c, (3a) * 26-5.3-106 (1.5) ** specifically stated an emergency existed when my children were picked up from their mother. After I (the father) was contacted and advised that my children would be returned to me after the court review there was no more emergency. Except per Colorado Human Resource Statement only. My home state report further verified this.
<u>Charge</u> ** (c) Human Service code 26-5.5-102 (a), (b), (d)** specifically stated; over involvement with unnecessary, unwarranted, and unsubstantiated retention of my children. The greatest degree of family structure was not followed. The most expensive and disruptive method was used and vigorously pursued by Human Resource Agency.

<u>Charge</u> ** (d) Human Service Code * 26-5-102 (1f), (2)*this section has been particularly violated in seeking to persuade my children
26-5.5-104 (1) ** specifically stated; violation of the
Legislative declaration and failure to use federal funds consistent to implement a family preservation program with applicable federal mandates. This would include restoring my children to me the father as a reunited family.

<u>Charge</u> ** (e) attempting to cover their actions by charging me (the father) with untrue acts in the courts.

Per *** abandoned my children, subjected my children to abuse or mistreatment. Suffered or allowed another to mistreat or abuse my children without taking lawful means to stop such and to prevent it in the future. Lack of proper parental care. Fail to provide education, medical care or other necessary care for my children. It is my understanding that once these charges are labeled in court, whether guilty or not, they will never leave your record and will follow you every where you; go until death

<u>Charge</u> ** (f) Human Services Code * 26-5.3-102 (b),
26-5.5-104 (3b) specifically stated; failure to provide adequately as to my children's cultural and ethnic background. This has resulted in my children being subjected to great verbal abuse. Failure to curb these attacks would be considered a hate crime in our home state. My children must now bring back to me a legacy of being cited for speaking their culture. Three of my children have begun showing anger, resentment, and violence in defending themselves. This trait has arisen only since being in foster care. Now ***** has began showing the beginning of asserting himself. This deterioration in such a short time is serious to me and should be to you.

<u>Charge</u> ** (g) ** shift of blame in failing efforts to me, the father, ********
*** The County has used these words to attempt to vilify me. Inference of inability to understand ** mental abuse ** age discrimination ** child abuse ** spousal abuse ** fear ** physical ** maltreatment ** abandoned **injurious** not taking responsibility ** denial ** verbal discipline ** yelling ** health problems ** may not be able to care for the children. ** and several other key words. In addition to these, they still count the calls to **********. As being against me and have never considered that I was living in the ****** facility during that time and that those calls were where the family was living. This is an ***** owned building. I did not go on the premises. ***** paid the bills. It appears that speculation and not facts is the preference of Jefferson County in these matters at some times.

Requested remedy.***** immediate return of my children; returned to my custody. There is no longer an emergency situation existing. I have neglected none of my children. ******* has released full authority to me. There is no need for out of home care since all provision is made for them under my care. This has always been the case. Whether at the **** or at the **** special housing has always been maintained for the children. The only reason they are out of home is because Jefferson County has decided it. My charge is that Jefferson County has not sought the proper return because the aid can be provided for one year. I maintain that the program set forth by Jefferson County is not what is needed but to gain what is given The County as per code 26-5.3-105 (2)

I believe that every child should be paid one thousand dollars for each day they spend separated from their family in violation of both your state and federal mandates. I also hold that two thousand dollars a day be paid to each child in punitive damages for all the stress, strain, humiliation, and intimidation that they have suffered and are suffering daily. I extend this same financial charge for the sister ***, who has been found crying many days over the fact that her brothers and sisters are not with her. At times her greatest fear is that The County will not return them to us. Her sorrow has kept her up many nights. Both myself and above all these five children should not have to go through such agony in a system that is supposed to unite, not look for a way to divide. No father should be slapped in the face and told how terrible he is because he is seeking to be a man for his family. Thanks

ONCE INSIDE THE SYSTEM

Every door to your children may be locked. You may be accused ignored, rejected. Lied on, humiliated, and nothing can be or will be done. You can be and may be totally cut off from all contact or communication with your children whether it is legal or illegal on the hostages keepers part **** Unless you have big bucks. Follow the letter pattern and wonder if you can protect your child. In spite of laws, codes, federal, state, local, or otherwise the system was not moved. Facts, questions, emergencies, lies, injustice, sexual abuse, verbal abuse, and racial abuse, within the system did not move the system. Higher authority was like a song and a dance. Law enforcement agencies stood on the sidelines and said, who me?

Outside this Human Resource System, you and I could be jailed for the injustices but inside this system appeared to be an untouchable group of lawbreakers toward our children. This pattern must be changed. No child must ever again be allowed to be shut off from a parent in America and placed in involuntary slavery by a state or government system. A parent without rights is a heritage without rights. A heritage without rights is a nation without rights. Why resist an overseas dictator when you have several in authority inside your own American system?

Can you imagine a child denied any contact with his parents? Can you imagine a child when they do talk to the parents having every conversation monitored by a trained professional? Can you imagine the professional having a mandate from The County that every child twelve years or older must be counseled with the intent to persuade them to say yes to whatever plan set before them by The County?

Can you imagine every child taken into custody as a foster parent child being at the same time placed in an adoption home with The County having a right to place your child in that home permanently based on their attachment to your child in their assigned time there? Can you imagine Parent Care being a part of an Adoption Scheme? A legal door to take your child and fill an adoption request?

In this chapter, I have placed a copy of some of the letters that I wrote and mentioned some of my call inquiries. It is interesting to note that of my written letters, all of the Civil Rights inquiry persons answered me. All offered advice but all declined to help. Washington Civil Rights Office and Human Resource Office answered after several weeks. One California Senator answered in a timely manner. Most of my letters were unanswered. The names of the persons and agencies are not included. This book was almost completed at the time of this incident. This book represents excerpts from over thirty-four years of involvement in counseling and advising those who were involved with The Human Resource, Social Service or Welfare area. Publication was delayed that this book also should become a personal documentary and a limited instruction manual for those concerned about the freedom of their children and others. A Civil Rights Case has been filed.

18. WHO WILL RESCUE MY CHILD? WHO? (DOCUMENTARY)

SENT TO SEVERAL CIVIL RIGHTS ADVOCATES FOR } REVIEW PACKET FOR REVIEW WAS INCLUDED WITH THE LETTER

I am writing in hopes of possible review and any assistance that you may be able to give. I have sought to give you all information that I have and my action with the court. I have been attempting to file a Civil Rights suit since April. I think that the last paperwork needed was sent last week. *********is my Civil Rights lawyer. Great knowledge. I understand that this may be the first Family Civil Rights lawsuit of this kind per Children so we need all the help that we can get. After talking to over fifteen lawyers I found that most run from Civil Rights and Children involved cases. I started this on my own but was laughed at and totally ignored. ***** rescued me.

My four children have been in foster care in Colorado since ******** I have a clean record per my standard and have been cleared by their home inspection. Yet they refuse to give my children to me.

None of my children have changed their statements to me but each hearing something new is being given to the court. I did hire a Colorado lawyer per their disdain of my statements but I do not expect much from Colorado. I believe only a Civil Rights win will stop the practice of children retention in an unlawful manner and scorn for the law as it is written. Thanks for this review and consideration.

WRITTEN TO MY LAWYER AFTER HUMAN RESOURCES HAD PROMISED FOR THE FOURTH TIME TO RELEASE PART OF MY CHILDREN

I will be there to pick up my children. I need to know the time and date they will be released to me.

You mentioned what is their accusation of me being in denial. I have asked them the same thing several times. This is a blanket term they are using to inject whatever they think is appropriate at the time. There is no specific denial. My   letters in the packet you have been sent explains my answer. There is nothing else to say. Truth is truth. My children are being held in violation of the code used by Colorado and the code used by The Federal Government. I have been cleared by their home study. The******** said they could release them to me but chose not to. The Human Service witness were not sworn in and the ******said they did not have to swear them in. My girls are not allowed to speak to us without being monitored. ***** was threatened to be put in a woman's jail until she began talking their talk in December. My girls have been intimidated and accusations of sexual abuse have been brought against the Human Service placement while there. To protect their reason for keeping my children in their facility, a campaign has been waged against me to degrade my ability and character. As a lawyer familiar with these cases and a file in your hands you know it is wrong and they should have released my children to me in ********   as a junior historian, I call their actions Gestapo tactics, mind control, defamation of character, alienation from the laws of America, denial of freedom of speech, incarceration without commission of a crime, denial of the right to raise a family in the life, liberty, and pursuit of happiness, denial of a father to exercise his role as a guide, counselor, provider, educator, denial of free speech within a family, invasion of privacy, unlawful separation of a family, labeling a parent guilty until proven innocent, using the family case excuse to exercise a dictator type power of families which come to their attention in their county, making speculation a foundation of their authority and Civil, Federal, and Family Law, disdain for the American Constitution, and an atmosphere that this branch is untouchable in its actions.

This is a partial result of some of my research.

I will appear by phone this time. I have made provision to arrive there within a day to pick up my children when released. I will be at my home phone ******

If the time is still at*** A.M. your time, I will be here. I will call about ** A.M. Make sure I have the number. My cell number is ****court date *** is this right???

Thanks for your service. I do look forward to picking up my children. Your efforts have been most helpful.

thanks. Note** the court would not let me appear by phone as they had in the past. Thanks

SENT TO SEVERAL OF OUR NEWSPAPER FRIENDS FOR YOUR INFORMATION AND REVIEW

I have four children in custody in Jefferson County Colorado being held in foster care. My term is that they are being held as A Hostage Of The State by reason of violation of The Human Services Code, Civil Rights Code, Colorado Human Service Code, Federal Funding Mandate, and Colorado Legislature Mandate.

I have enclosed a copy of the statutes that I believe have been openly violated which was presented to The Social Services, Family Court and The Commissioners that I understand oversee this phase of Colorado Government. A copy has also been sent to Colorado Elected Officials in some areas.

If violation of Civil Rights is so matter of fact in this case, it tells me that it must be very common and many other families are affected but too poor, fearful, or ignorant of the law to protest with a meaningful voice.

You are part of a free voice. Multitudes of innocent children and parents can suffer if this example of Civil Rights Violations of The Child And Parent is performed on a regular basis. I have begun to initiate a lawsuit for The Civil Rights of these children and my own Civil Rights as a parent. American residents should seek justice for their family's and neighbors. God given justice in America is our right. It has been legislated, and mandated. Let us enforce it justly.Thanks for listening. Stay informed on this case of Civil Rights The Children and Family. Thanks

LETTER TO ******** IN REFERENCE TO SON BORN OUT OF WEDLOCK TARGETED FOR ADOPTION BY COLORADO AGENCY

In reference to ******* the son of ********* and the brother of the present siblings in custody of the State of Colorado ** specifically identified in the following case ****. As the father of the present four children in Colorado State custody and having been cleared of any obstacle to the return of these natural children, I request custody of ******* along with the rest of the four. There is no other persons as qualified as the father and his sons and daughters to provide a home for this new arrival into the family.

To refuse to unite ***** with his family in the home setting that is presently waiting for him is to violate his rights according to The Human Service Code as well as the brothers, sisters, and verified family.

To even suggest that ****** and my girls should be placed in a different setting than The Human Service Code and The Civil Rights Code mandates is a horrible thought that is downright Anti American.

Both of these codes declare that the family is the foundation of America. This is what should be. I am requesting **** be reunited with my children and I.

Thanks

LETTER TO OFFICE OF CIVIL RIGHTS WASH. D.C.*** SAME LETTER TO ADMINISTRATION OF CHILDREN SERVICES IN WASH. D. C.

Charge ** violation of Human Service Code as set forth by The State of Colorado legislative declaration and applicable Federal Mandates.

In the enclosed petition, I have set forth my objective statements and suggested remedy.

I do not have five thousand dollars to hire a lawyer and my doubt is high on which lawyer to obtain in Colorado because so many of the family lawyers have a contract with Social Services or other County and State Connected Agencies. I have been advised that because of the urgency and the deterioration of my children in foster care to begin by filing this petition myself. This I have done.

It may be possible that a specific form may be required by a specific court. If this is so, I request that this form be waived in favor of speedy resolution of an already time stretched case. I do believe that there is no emergency need as to provisions of my children being available in my home. There is an emergency in Colorado being willing to get them home to me.

I have submitted this petition to Jefferson County and at the same time I am seeking information in case I must seek to either The District or Federal Court. Time is of essence and damage has been done. If there are forms or procedures that I must follow, please submit them to me, by Overnight, Express, or FedEx. I will reimburse you for your expense immediately.

I request immediate action to avoid further damage to my children. Noticeable damage *****
***** ** becoming more assertive and willing to be aggressive in defending her principles. *** small periods of slight depression which I consider very dangerous considering her fragile personality. School problems and depression may increase.
******** several fights and suspensions have occurred and will possibly accelerate as her will is not being counseled through close father contact and communication.
**** ** severe depression signs have appeared hidden by his usual reserved quietness. ** willingness to defend his principles with physical force if physically challenged.
**** ** first stages of assertiveness

All of these conditions have begun since they were placed in foster care. None of these conditions would exist if they had been reunited with me as your Colorado Code provides. Both State and Federal mandates have been violated whether in ignorance or willful practice. It is possible to correct this error today.

I am certain that you are not aware of the routine practice of any program using borderline practices to obtain maximum grants or you would intervene. The open blatant violation of The Human Resource Code and extremely obvious misuse of Federal funds totally surprised me. To hear people discuss it and never seek to correct it makes me wonder how corrupt can a County System be or how wrong am I.

One of the most disturbing occurrences has been the violation of our Civil Rights. While discussing the problem with some of our Colorado Lawyers, I found it hard to believe what I was told to expect from Jefferson

County Family Services. I considered it all heresy. But the facts seem to be following the pattern that I was told to expect. First, maximum retention of the children. Second, finding some fault with the parent so they could not be reunited even if the placement is with another family member. Third, finding a reason to cut communication with the child. Fourth, find a reason to declare abandonment for long time retention.

Colorado has violated our Civil Rights according to the full findings of congress in Civil Rights Code 12301 with 7e and 7f questionable.

Colorado has labeled atrocious charges against me per a court summons received by fax in San Jose on January Third with at least two dates on it. Colorado has denied a reunited family though cleared by the requested California Home study.

A paper was included in the files which the judge had not seen on the day of conversation. The writer and I had one ten to fifteen minute phone talk. I was told there was no problem my boys could be returned anytime. When I received the paper that was given to the court it was a total stranger being talked about. How can you give an opinion on things never mentioned or discussed? That paper was basically written to belittle. Not to be completely factual.

If this is being done to me today, how many more was it done to that did not or could not raise their voice due to fear, lack of funds to obtain a lawyer not tied to The Colorado Local System, for fear their children would not be returned. Colorado should be open for a class action review of their past cases and appropriate action as needed.

To hear these practices informationally, I was naïve.

 as a part of these practices, I am now convinced.

My children are A Hostage to The State Of Colorado by virtue of Jefferson County Human Services.

I request you review these facts and adjust accordingly. If I have erred in the application of the codes, please enlighten me.

Again time is of essence. My children are being harmed mentally and being placed in a position to fight for themselves is harming even their reputation. Colorado is using a word game to destroy the will, lifestyle, and character of my family. Why should any branch of Human Services become a dictator or oppressor of certain people or families? Enclosed is my documented answer to this injustice. I trust that you can and will correct it immediately. Thanks ****** ******

SENT TO GOVERNOR OF CUSTODY STATE

You oversee thousands and it is easy to miss a comma or a period with so many letters. My normal complaint would seem regular except that I have spent thirty-four years dealing with similar cases and have never seen such disregard and such a risk to speak or twist facts in error. It has taken from over one year and cost over 9 thousand dollars just to receive the first promise to investigate this case.

Last year ago   ** plus, two of my children asked me if they ran away would I pick them up? In checking, I was told that if they ran away, they would be arrested and I would be arrested for aiding them. I spoke to all my children and advised properly. I do consider my children Hostages Of The State Of Colorado.

I could be wrong.**** I have enclosed the packet that I presented originally, as I reviewed The Colorado Code. Stating the errors and wrongs would seem like a fantasy, star wars type drama, no way in the world could I believe it. *** please review and correct this situation. Thanks What is being done to my children must be occurring to many others.

SENT TO CALIFORNIA GOVERNOR UPON SUGGESTION OF A SENATOR

I am writing you upon the suggestion of Senator ***** I am not sure how the Senator became aware of the situation. Senator *** may have been notified by myself or one of my sympathizers.

The story is so unrealistic, I would find it hard to believe if I were not directly involved.
Therefore I have submitted to you the packet I sent to the ***** Governor seeking a solution.
Is it possible that you could help promote a solution?
Thanks for taking time in your multitude of duties to consider one family's well being.
Thanks greatly

LETTER SENT TO COLORADO DEPT.

I was advised to contact you by The Washington D. C. Office.

Due to the conflicting words that I have received in the last two weeks, I thought it better that I send you a copy of my complaints and charges. This is only the original complaints and charges. This is only the original complaints presented to the agency and the courts based on the Colorado Code and The Congress Affirmed Civil Rights. This is not the Civil Rights Suit now being investigated.

Two weeks ago, my boys told me they were coming home on the **** of *** in talking to the social worker
They stated my boys would be released around the court date of ***** I planned to pick them up around that date. I talked to the social worker on *** and was given around ****. With this date, they would be put on a plane. I have been given money to fly them home at that date. I talked to my lawyer this morning. On the *** he told me the court paper said the social worker had recommended my boys stay in your custody. What is the truth? Court date is ***
My charges are many against this agency.

The social worker told me on *** that she is not aware of some of my complaints and charges. I did not inform her. She was not clear on whether or not she would recommend releasing my girls to me at this time. She said the judge would make the final decision. My lawyer said her recommendation was dated on the ***prior to her talking to me. I am submitting my Colorado Code complaints to you. You may not be aware either. My original notification of complaint was in *** a copy of the Colorado Code of Human Service is included.
The damage done can never be repaired. Yet I see no willingness to correct the future. Hopefully I am wrong in this vision. If I am right, thousands of homes will be destroyed by an agency created to help them. Cancer is a group of healthy cells gone wrong. We should represent the restorers of the breach. Every cancer cell should tremble. Set the hostage free. Thanks.

EXCERPTS FROM LETTER TO COLORADO AFTER INDITEMENT SENT TO ME IMMEDIATELY A COUPLE OF HOURS AFTER MY OFFICE INFO REQUEST

On ******* a document was completed giving me full physical custody of my children. You had assured me several times that you were doing a home study on me to verify that my children would be sent home to me. You emphasized that I did not have to come to Colorado but that you would put my children on a plane and send them to me. I was assured that a home study request had been sent. On ****, I contacted our office to see if the request had arrived. I gave the office a number to call. A couple of hours later you faxed an inditement accusing me of abandoning my children and allowing mistreatment without taking action to prevent it, etc.

This makes me question your truthfulness and your motives. You certainly did not consult with the court investigators, police dept, drug unit and child welfare unit before issuing your statements. You may consider their decision in error, but you appear to be on the verge of making a greater error if you don't accept their decision and handle this matter justly and truthfully. <u>Emotional abuse there has never been domestic violence by me.</u> I don't hit women unless it is accidental. I was not in that house on the days in question the emotional abuse came from my preaching two sermons against adultery, alcohol, and drugs. The social worker called me and advised me to change my sermons. <u>Afraid of me.</u> My children never said that. <u>Kicking is like profanity to me.</u> It has never been a part of me. I have been listening to that statement since over seven years and still don't remember it.

***** <u>was spanked on her hand.</u>

<u>Expedited home study.</u> It was signed on *****, signed again on ***** but had not got to office by ****. <u>Petition dependency or neglect.</u> None of these things happened while my children were in my custody. Why was I accused? <u>Too old to care for my children.</u> My girls did not say that. I must point out that at a later time this same statement was made and another person was supposedly raising the same question at that time who is really making the accusation? Why are pages one and four dated at a different time? When was this document created?

<u>LETTER TO COMMISSIONERS OVERSEEING COLORADO OFFICE-THREE COMMISSIONERS</u>

A directive was sent though your office to investigate a series of complaints regarding the safety of my children and the reunification of my children with me, the father. The instructions stated that I was to be notified in writing and a copy was to be sent to your complaint coordinator by ********as of ***** no report has been received.

I have been told by your social workers that it is my children's request to stay in foster care. And not return home. Why have my children not told me that? To further complicate matters, the last two times that I talked to my children, there was a fear in them. Where did the fear come from? Why are they never allowed to talk to me without being monitored? Why have instructions been ignored which basically have originated from Washington D.C. And The Senate? Why was a conversation relayed to me last week about the possibility of my children being harmed while in your care? Is there a possibility or a reason that my children are being treated as Hostages By The State of Colorado Human Service System? What danger could they be facing? I do await your answer speedily. Thanks

LETTER AFTER RECEIVING INFORMATION CALL FROM COLORADO

I sent you an overnight packet this morning. However, since returning to my office and reviewing my information, I thought it expedient to send you a fax since the **** is ****. I could not see a reason for the double talk or the shuffleboard tactics in giving out information to either my lawyer, my children or myself.

Since my girls have been involved in sexual activity since being in your care, and this was kept hidden from me for some time, the worst fears came to mind, as I reviewed the paperwork. I considered why no phone contact, why every call monitored, why threats to change their mind, why my girls, also boys are afraid to speak openly before their guardians, why such great effort and risk of job loss in relying on lies and double talk. After reviewing the files, I have not just a concern but also a fear for the safety of my children.

May haps my thirty four years counseling these areas of child concerns have given me too much knowledge, nevertheless **** the fear *** it is there. A copy of this letter was faxed to my lawyer.

AGENCIES CALLED AND THEIR RESPONSE AFTER RECEIVING A CALL FROM COLORADO ABOUT OVERHEARING A CONVERSATION ABOUT THE POSSIBILITY OF MY CHILDREN HARMING THEMSELVES. THESE CALLS WERE MADE AFTER NOT BEING ABLE TO REACH A HUMAN SERVICE REPRESENTATIVE.

The request was to send a third party to talk to my children without a monitor and request the reason for fear if it was present and to confirm that my children had chosen to stay in foster care by their request as the social worker had said several times.

<u>FBI</u> ******* we don't do that. Call the state police

<u>State police</u> **** we cant do that we only handle road patrol in the state. Call the sheriff department.

<u>Sheriff Office</u> *** we cant do that. Call The Social Welfare department.

<u>Called for information only</u>. <u>What do federal marshals do?</u> Deal with federal prisoners.

<u>INQUIRY LETTER TO COMPLAINT COORDINATOR</u>

Enclosed is a copy of your request for investigation of my inquiries and complaints dated ****, to date I have not heard such an answer. During my last two conversations with them, I question why were my girls so fearful? I have been told continually that my girls have opted to stay in foster care in Colorado rather than return home. Why have my girls not told me? Why have I been told that prisoners are monitored by their system so why should I worry about Human Service monitoring. This statement by your staff tells me that my children are really considered prisoners by your system.

Why did I receive a call from Colorado last week advising me that there is no way that your staff intends to release my girls to me regardless of what any home study or report says? Why was I told that the plan is to in any way possible adopt my girls out but keep them from me the father? Was my information wrong or did my source hear right? Why did I hear that a discussion occurred about the possibility of my children hurting themselves? Are my children in danger with your Colorado system? They are still being held illegally per my code and law investigation.

<u>ON ***** AN ELECTRONIC AFFIRMATION OF A CIVIL RIGHTS CASE WAS GIVEN FROM ***. LATER THE SAME DAY A COLORADO REPORT WAS SENT TO MY LAWYER IN COLORADO. THIS IS A PARTIAL RECORD OF THE ANSWER TO THAT REPORT</u>

Neither *** or *** said they were afraid of me. Neither ** or ** said I had glaucoma or a heart condition. I have never had either. Neither ** or *** has ever made reference to my age and ability to care for four children. Both report this as a lie by The Social Services.

*** denies making a statement that I hit her in front of my children. I understand at this time that this statement may have been reaffirmed.

At age five three of the children were playing house. They were adjusted and The Foster Care Persons, Child Welfare and The Police told me that this was not considered sexual abuse because they were the same age and all willing participants. My task was to instruct them and teach them properly. This I did. *** has been pressured to change his mind about living with me. He was rebuked by the social worker when he attempted to talk to me but still told me the story anyhow. He was pressured to write a letter and also explained to me why and what his true feelings are.

The fear factor is being pushed by the Human Service department as a reasonable cause to hold my children. None of my children has either shown or expressed fear of returning home with me. The therapy sessions per the conversation with my children have been to turn their thoughts from living with me and toward remaining in Colorado awaiting *** change.

The term physical abuse, sexual abuse, and spousal abuse have been raised since my children have been held in Colorado. In my case none of these are substantiated. It is a brainwashing technique that if a person hears a word often enough, they will believe it. These are not sworn statements. The *** said on *** hearing *** did not swear in the witness because they work for the agency. The statement was made that they could release my boys to me if they chose but they chose not to.

a   My children are being held as Jefferson County Hostages since *** The Civil Rights Code and The Family Service Code directed by Congress and The Colorado Legislature lists over twenty three violations in retaining these children. Jefferson County is technically not qualified to receive any federal funds and should have a federal review of all their cases and a class action lawsuit as to The Families Civil Rights that have been violated. Open lies, twisted words, and brainwashing techniques should be illegal in the United States Human Services Departments. We should not be Gestapo's with the mentality to keep your child to the maximum extent possible as long as government pays.

b   None of my children fear punishment. My children are instructed each time I talk to them to tell the truth. Do not allow themselves to be persuaded to do anything but tell the truth and serve God. Pray and remember they will always wear their own name. Do not be ashamed of their past. It can be changed from today on. Live perfect and right from today on. On *** as I began to talk to my children, I asked them why the therapist said they change their statements so often. When I began speaking to them to always tell the truth, *** became very upset and took the phone and rebuked me heavily. ** said it is not my children but it is me. I have to confess my wrong and stop my denial. I am the wrong one. I am guilty, I must acknowledge my guilt. It is not the children. My children have been programmed. They are not afraid of me. They are afraid of irritating their keepers or therapist. They changed their statements when they were reminded to always tell the truth.

c   This is a repeat of the words sexual abuse, domestic violence, and spousal abuse. It did not happen but repetition plants the thought and idea. The accusations are being planted throughout the report so the readers will not miss it. It is again a brainwashing technique used by many. *** did not make that accusation.

Why should a person admit something that he did not do? This is guilty because I say so. Innocent until proven guilty is The Law of Civil Rights. Why am I presumed guilty until proven innocent?

In the matter of protection. Why have it not been mentioned that my girls were sexually abused while in the care of The Foster Parents in Colorado? *** why have they not mentioned that my girls have been racially abused while in the care of Colorado Jefferson County Human Services? Why have they not mentioned that right now they have put *** on a medication which have caused bleeding for over four months? Why have they not mentioned that they put my daughter on a medication that has caused her weight to accelerate to over one hundred ninety pounds? Why have they not mentioned that they have cut my communication with my children and even when my daughter had an emergency it took me eleven phone calls and over eighteen hours to get her checked for a condition which has life threatening symptoms for her when it occurs? Why have they not mentioned that the therapist said it took my daughter over four months to get her to say anything negative about me? I ask the question. Did it take this long to tell the truth or did it take that long for the brain washing technique to begin working?

My children have never changed their statements to me since being in Colorado. Why does every report that I read from the court have a bunch of new allegations and issues which means that truth is being distorted?

WRITTEN AFTER RECEIVING LETTER FROM DENVER OFFICE OF CIVIL RIGHTS THAT CASE WOULD BE DROPPED.

I received a letter today that the complaint is being dropped for lack of some paperwork. I have not been able to contact Denver yet so this letter may be pre mature. It will not be dropped by me. We are now major victims of the vilest possible attacks that The Human Services could possibly label against a father and his family. I did not believe such vile attacks were possible in a Government Funded Program in America today. Time is of essence. A Civil Rights Suit has and is being filed. Thanks

I do consider it very interesting that two of the most serious inditements against me were received immediately after either a phone call from my state or an electronic complaint filing from my state.

Tell me, oh man, standing by the sea
Have you seen a lost girl or boy?
No old man, I have not seen either.
But I did see a small shoe and a broken toy.

Was the toy a doll? A little teddy bear?
Was it a musical toy? A small guitar?
You guessed it old man. It was a white teddy bear.
Please help me search, they can't be very far.

Sorry old man, I must check on my home.
Darkness is falling, it is getting quite late.
But sir, your home is safe, my children are lost.
Quite true old one, that is your fate.

19. HOSTAGE TAKERS ****
DEFEND YOUR GROUND

THE DOCUMENTARY CONTINUES

One year has now passed. Numerous accusations have been made against me. The investigation has cleared me to receive my children. **** but there is now a difference. I am fighting back. Why? This situation involves thousands of children. The hostage at will without a voice must be stopped. My humiliation and disrespect as a parent is as deadly to me as the evil that killed three northerners that dared to speak up for the rights of the oppressed in the south. This is the same disrespect that buried a fourteen-year-old boy in a southern river. This is a part of American Government refusing to abide by its own laws and the laws of America. My Family's Civil Rights must be restored and with them the rights of every mother and father in America with the rights of every child protected as The Constitution states.

Can an agency be fair in its own investigation? No parent should be ashamed or afraid to stand for the decency of teaching honor, dignity, respect, for your home, society, and The Eternal God and the thought and ambition that you can and will succeed in every area you turn to. So a visit from one of my Colorado opponents was welcomed with great expectation. I even missed one day of a Leadership Conference that I was to minister in for this unusual honor. This usually doesn't happen. My only reservation was that this should have happened over a year ago when my children were first made A Hostage Of The State and well before A Civil Rights Suit was filed.

My suspicion (if I let it rule) would be that this was not a simple home or fact-finding mission but a find a fault to prove us right mission. One year later looking for a reason was too late for the trauma, turmoil, and confusion that was injected into my home by an agency created to unite **** not divide.

My home state did notify me that they had been requested to do another home study. This did not surprise me. I did ask if they were prompted toward any particular areas. They simply stated that some specific areas were pointed out. This was expected. The home study team had spent two weeks investigating before I obtained a letter from Colorado. It had been sent to my ministry address and the label was not legible. I received it in time for the third week review.

A new home study was requested under the guise that over six months had elapsed and the study was mute. I was informed that Colorado had asked for several things. This was all right with me. I considered the request a Colorado defense play after the game had ended over a year ago. I also considered that this could still be another ploy to maintain control over my children. It could be an attempt to go through another two to three month session at a time which a judge collaborating with a system could implement under the guise of further investigation.

As one adviser put it. "Reverend, you have challenged their system." He said," "They will be as slow and stubborn as they can be to show you that you are nothing and they are still in control." I listened to his theory but I will never accept it as a valid theory to implement if The Human Resource Department Of Civil Service is really about children's well being.

We have all heard stories but this writing is intended to show facts concerning our children that are literal prisoners or Hostages Of The State. These facts are true based. Let freedom sing because someone cares. Let no child ever again be held a state prisoner for over a year, before the reason he or she is there is investigated.

The first question asked. Why were you in a dumpster in 1991 at 12 a.m. at night with your oldest daughter in your car? My answer, **** ask me under oath in a court and I will tell you. My daughter was two years old at that time. Second question, Colorado is requesting that you take a psychological evaluation. My answer; If my president The Honorable George W. Bush will take such an evaluation on why he is fighting a war on terror in Iraq or my third favorite talk show host Mr. Heraldo Rivera take such an evaluation on why he comes up with so many **** unique statements then I will take one with them. I refuse. Why should I have to take such a thing when the social workers don't even have to be sworn in? Besides the law is plain. It was violated and used against me, not by me. In this situation, an agency is the violator.

** just for the record, I am not anti Bush or Rivera **

Third question, List of all my biological children and info on them. My answer. That is irrelevant. This is about my minor children and our home. Fourth question, On occasion I had reported that I had 9 children. That is true. At times I reported that I had from I to 12 children. None were twins. Fifth question, am I going to get married? My answer, "Yes. The background check is complete on the guaranteed person. He has been called a lawyer and does a great job in pleading my case. I recommend that this question be deleted. You would probably not accept my complete answer." Sixth question, Prior relationships and marriages or unions? My answer, "not applicable to my present family." "Not relevant and an invasion of privacy." Seventh question. What is my employment? My answer, "I am a minister. I work for no salary." Eighth question. What about the children you cared for in your home? My answer, " Too many to count." Ninth question. What about a parenting class that I took and the facilitator recommended that I take an additional year after taking sixteen weeks? <u>My answer, "If they knew that much, they knew that I was not ordered to take that class." "I requested it and had to literally fight to get into it." "They also received the report that was given to the agency and it is chapter (36) page 85 (titled) Court ordered training ** It may not be for you Afro American in the book AFDC, Cadillac And Child Support, Let My People Go." "I wrote a story.</u>" "I gave a report to an agency." "What they did with it was their business." Tenth question, were my children ever interviewed in my presence by Social Service? No! Question eleven, what about hurt or damage through their life experience? My answer, " That was not the question or the issue stated by the therapist." Question twelve, what problems do I see the children having while in Colorado care? My answer, "my children are being denied their Family Rights both Natural and Civil per Colorado Human Service Code, Colorado State Assembly Code, United States Congress Civil Code, and The Constitution Of The United States Of America Civil Rights violation." "They are virtual prisoners under a foster care name." Question thirteen, What about a claim that I harmed my girls? My answer, " This is not applicable." "It is only promoted by Colorado." "Ask me in a court under oath not overseen by Human Service if you are unsatisfied with these answers."

I received a copy of these questions in letters from Colorado on ******. They were sent to the wrong address and the label was not legible. I typed these answers in my office Sunday night. They were typed as I reviewed the paperwork sent from Colorado.

I have serious reservations about the request for a second home study. Colorado wrote my home state near the first of October asking them why they were requesting that I take a psychological evaluation as part of a second home study. My home state told me that Colorado asked for the home study and evaluation. Colorado's letter was dated twenty three days after their letter of inquiry to my home state. Is there an error in communication in the camp? What is the purpose? Honesty and truth travels one road. Who really asked for the evaluation? Which state? An unknown person from a meeting in which it was stated that California Social Service had suggested that I was mentally unstable sent documentation to me from Colorado. I did contact the California Office. I was informed that there had been no communication to that effect at that time. It did come later. My question was, did Colorado attempt to set me up as a crazy man? The paperwork leans toward yes, yes, yes.

Question nine is answered in the chapter (fall out)

All of mankind has made many mistakes.
Often, we have stood with our backs to the wall.
Still, this is not the issue that troubles us most.
It is our success. Will we stand or fall?

We struggle so often wrestling with truth.
Should we hold truth up or lift up a lie.
When the sun sets, truth is still standing.
When it rises again, truth is still there. Why, why?

Truth is one thing that never changes.
Truth will reign throughout eternity.
Truth will carry the truthful on its shoulders,
With the resounding cry, they are free, free, free.

Why are children excluded from the process?
Why are they used as a liar's tool?
Why are they denied both hope and freedom?
Why does a state say they must live as a fool?

20. FAMILY CIVIL RIGHTS ***
THESE HAVE BEEN FOUGHT FOR ***
THEY HAVE ALREADY BEEN WON ***

Churchill won because he said England would never quit. England rallied behind him. His country backed freedom and fought oppression. American freedom began in homes across the sea and continued in our land as family freedom was pursued. Have we fallen asleep? Are we not aware that thousands of our children are being enslaved illegally every day by our system and thousands of our parents are victims of oppression of our rights. Do we know that our Civil Rights As Families have been well defined by the courts? Do we know that many of the parent's children that have been removed have been removed illegally or are being retained illegally against The Parent and Child's Civil Rights?

The scorn and disdain for Family Civil Rights has and is destroying thousands of American Families. The statement, I know what the law says but it is negotiable. I can change it if I choose represents a Dictator, Vigilante, Nazi, Ku Klux Klan spirit. This statement coming from a Human Resource supervisor destroys the credibility of one charged to oversee our needy families. The fact that the agency defends the practice implies that the agency has sold out its agency credibility. This spirit must be challenged and defeated.

Our children and homes must be governed by the laws of freedom and democracy, not whims or speculation. Are your Family Civil Rights being violated? You correct it. When The State Courts fail to protect your family per their Constitutional duty, it is or should be the duty of The Federal Courts or Government to intervene. <u>America does not need a government that will guarantee the freedom of other nations and allow the destruction of its own families.</u>

The following is a small list of Parental and Children Civil Rights that are being violated daily. These areas are victories proven and won in America's courts. These are Civil Rights that we should not have to suffer for. Read them and claim them. Your law libraries across America carry the court cases that have been fought and won supporting this small list of Civil Rights. Use this small group as a foundation stepping-stone. Fight for Your Family, and Your Children's Civil Rights. Begin the freedom march for your family.

1. <u>Every parent has a constitutional and fundamental right to custody of their children.</u>
2. <u>In order to lose custody of your children there must be clear showing of gross neglect, unfitness, extra ordinary circumstances of misconduct on the part of the parents to affect the children.</u>
3. <u>To lose custody of your children, a parent must abandon the children or forfeit their parental rights. This must be verified by the agency taking the children. *** most courts advise a person to sign with the question do you understand? Ninety nine percent don't know what they are doing.</u>
4. <u>Every parent has Natural and Legal rights to the custody of their children. Nothing should be signed. If you are wrong, it is not necessary to sign. Your signature is often used to declare that you consented to the action.</u>
5. <u>To lose custody of your children, there must be a preponderance of evidence against a parent. The standard of proof has been referred to as clear, clear and conclusive, plain and certain, strong and satisfactory, cogent and convincing, substantial, or clear and convincing.</u>
6. <u>You cannot lose custody unless there is a threat by the parent to the welfare or safety of the children or the children are a threat to the public in any way.</u>
7. <u>Every parent has a constitutional right to the companionship, care, custody, and management of their children.</u>

8. A parent has both legally cognizable and substantial rights that may not be overridden in the absence of being unfit or unsuitable to be a parent.
9. Overt and subtle intimidation is illegal to be used to alienate a child's affection. This includes threats, promises, cultivating fear, distrust etc. Persuasion one way or another either by the state or out of home placement persons. This includes the trained professionals that are assigned to children over twelve to get them to agree to the agency plans.
10. Invasion of privacy. Every family has a right to private conversation with their family. Guaranteed by the fourteenth amendment.
11. State or agency burden to terminate parental rights.*** it must be proven by clear and convincing evidence, beyond a reasonable doubt, or by a preponderance of evidence.
12. State or agency burden must prove that transfer of the parent's rights to the agency is in the best interests of the children. Their mental, health, physical health, school and social areas must be better. Medical areas must benefit. Drug, alcohol, sexual abuse, sexual activity, violence, and juvenile activity now become the state or agency responsibility. You hold them accountable for your children. My latest statistics show the state is losing on the drug, alcohol, sexual activity, violence, and juvenile areas. The state and not the parent is the guilty when they have taken control under the guise that they are better able to control.
13. The constitution guarantees children a normal, unobstructed relationship with their parents.
14. Children are lacking in several areas of maturity and leadership, experience, counsel, and guidance in moral standards, good citizenships, and general decisions that are in their best interests
15. Parental rights are superior over that of minor children in nurture, and education and in areas of mitigating circumstances. This includes abuse, physical abuse, verbal abuse, drug activity, racial intimidation, sexual abuse, physical violence, and residence choice. A child's desire to live apart from a parent is still subject to a parental decision. A child is not mature enough to make a total life changing choice of this magnitude without a parent.
16. Parental authority is plenary and prevails over the claims of all minor children and over any agency that seeks to or does remove children from parental custody.

17. <u>The prevailing interest in the raising of children in America should be that they be raised without any type of state or government interference.</u>
18. <u>It is a Civil Rights violation for any parent or child to be denied a major life activity that has been granted under The Constitution Of The United States Of America. It is a common misconception that Civil Rights pertain only to race, job, voting, pay, housing, public policies, on gender, religion, etc.</u>

For me to find well over a hundred court cases defending Family Civil Rights within a couple of hours study at a law library was quite a shocker. My over thirty years of listening, counseling and not going to a law library for a thorough examination of the records tells me that every major city and county that has dealt with our children in custody and out of home placement, including adoption practices should be facing a class action suit from mistreated parents. Your child was not excluded from civil rights. Your complaints must be heard. Your case must be investigated. Your wrongs must be corrected. The multi-billion dollar business that was created by taking our children must be corrected.

Often the ones in the forefront of battle
Seem very reserved and shy.
They prefer to stay in the background,
But can't stand to see the helpless cry.

They often walk as an armor bearer,
Standing in the shadow of the oppressed.
Their counsel is often behind the lines.
In silence and secret they give many rest.

Now sometimes after the battle is over,
And we think all secrets are revealed,
The names of the background helpers.
Are published everywhere and unsealed.

I was once a background person.
Then someone leaked my name.
Instead of giving me the honor I deserved.

I was heaped with dishonor, lies, and shame.

I am now a frontline soldier.
I must fight today because of a war back then.
When I was a behind the scenes soldier.
A secret not always kept by men.

This chapter is included because of reference to two of my old behind the scenes activities

21. FALL OUT *********
LET ME EXPLAIN *******

<u>Question number one</u>, Why were you in a dumpster around 12 a.m. at night with your daughter in your car parked about five feet away? What they did not say or ask is why was I stopped on at least three other occasions and questioned because I had both black and white children in the car. There was at least one other non-black adult in the car each time. ****
Where were we? At a wholesale food distributor company. How often did we go there? Some of our ministers went there five nights a week after six. Usually between six thirty p.m. and two a.m. How often did I go there? It varied. Usually on Friday during all night prayer. I would go up to check the area and be an example for the ministers. What was the purpose?

How did this practice start? Our church was in downtown San Jose, California. The area was full of homeless at that time. Up to twenty plus persons slept on our pews in the church each night. On the weekends my living quarters was turned over to a neighbor lady (member of our church that housed the homeless minors.) I slept in the church on those days. Why? Her husband came into town on those nights.

The wholesale house ? Two of the employees were aware of our efforts. The warehouse inventory was purged once a month. They began leaving their outdated inventory on our doorstep. We had no idea who was leaving it or where it was coming from. We often done some of our buying at this wholesale house. Sometime later the employees told us as we shopped there that they were the ones leaving the items there but now if we wanted them we would have to pick them up at the warehouse. They gave us the dates of the purging and we began doing so.

Their reason: some began thinking they may be giving items that were not outdated. A third change. Same reason, almost: we were advised that the items had to be placed in the dumpster to insure that they were targeted to be thrown away. Would we object to getting them out of the dumpster? This was a little humiliating but since we were training preachers and had a live in group of trainees of from ten plus in addition to our sleep ins at night, we thought this was a great opportunity to both accept and teach humility in doing good.

This became one of our main humility teaching tools. Normally this would have been targeted as being racist, biased and a discriminatory, humiliating experience but because of our job of training preachers and leaders, we sought to turn it into an inspirational experience. It worked.

Later days same experience: one of the biggest donators to the food bank in our city last year was the ****** food chain. Several years ago, upon hearing of our food efforts to help the needy,***** invited us to pick up their outdated surplus. This we did. This was curtailed upon a management change. Upon a new management change, we were again given the privilege of picking up their surplus. This time it was after they placed the products inside their bins.

This was not food products only. Our efforts helped people from Santa Cruz, to Sacramento California. It included anything from hams and turkeys to flag poles, shaving cream, Baby food, deodorant, soap, toothpaste and pies. If it did not sell, we got a chance to give it away. When did it stop? The humility is still there or should I say still within our group. The contributions or should I say a major portion of the foodstuff is being distributed through a food bank program.

The complaints had began again when a couple of chef cooks and street vendors began complaining about the church that was picking up the items. We did share items with them freely. However, their main aim was to obtain the items for money while our aim was to help the needy. We distributed the items to the poor and needy without price. I like to think that because of our efforts a greater contribution has occurred. That food chain is now making a greater community contribution than ever before.

Question number one has a still greater message behind it. It is all good when spoken from my side. (the garbage can dive that fed thousands). Their side? Hear it under oath. Smile ** humiliation can be profitable *** we did not hang our head in shame, we lifted it high and fed the hungry and encouraged the hopeless.******

Question number nine.*** this episode has been published in my book, AFDC, Cadillac And, Child Support; Let My People Go. The chapter is titled ** Court Ordered Training, it may not be for you Afro American***

One of the services that was offered to church members and their friends was free baby-sitting if they needed it. Our church kept two cars that were available to a person needing transportation. They could borrow the cars as long as needed and if a driver was available, they could be driven to various destinations. If the cars did not suffice, we would keep their children for them. This was free unless they chose to donate to the church. At times, this service lasted for days and weeks depending upon their situation. We have had as high as thirty plus children at a time.

We were continually visited and monitored by various city, county, and state agencies. We went through their training but never accepted licensing by any agency. Our primary reason for this was that at that time we were told that if you carry our license, you obey all our regulations. If you don't carry our license, you are responsible for safety and health regulations only. This was a policy of our church and still is to help the poor and needy if we have the funds and means and can do it legally. Several areas were corrected from time to time per the inspections. At times, the inspections numbered as high as five a month. Often a policeman accompanied the social worker. Nothing illegal was ever found.

It was my practice to check with the Child Care, Police, and Social Service every year to see if there were any changes in the child care regulations. The number one rated Child Care Program   reportedly recommended by the court was a program that refused to let me attend voluntarily. It had to be court recommended or so they said. At the time, I was writing documentation for two books. AFDC, Cadillac, And Child Support, Let My People Go which was a true story book of economic, financial, sports, racial prejudice, etc. And ambition with success as the oppressed refused to be suppressed but rose to the top of success in various chosen areas.

The second book is the book that you are now reading. Children Hostage Of The State Innocent Prisoners Without A Trial. This book has been rewritten and the article has been slightly altered though not changed. A report was given to the system with a complaint about the obvious open opposition I received. I was not ordered to take this course but used the intimidation with a belt which was a former practice of mine at that time to enter the class.

This was a legal reason for my entry into the class even though it was over a year in the past and had been discarded due to rule change knowledge. My assigned social worker honored my request for entry and sent me to the program. My wife at the time was assigned to the class. There was a class for the men and also a class for women ** consider** the article *** the story *** chapter 36 in AFDC, Cadillac And Child Support Let My People Go.

Men at the top often are ignorant of the ground floor activities. This is what can happen when you send a black man to a program that is supposed to be the best in The Silicon Valley. This is the account as documented by myself. You decide whether or not it is pocket segregation. The first telephone call seemed simple enough. Bring in your paper work and since it is usually a co-share payment, bring in your fee and we will schedule you for the class. When I went in for the registration, the young lady told me that the papers were not sufficient and she could not take my money or register me at that time. I asked what she needed and informed the proper social worker of the necessary papers. These papers were faxed to the office post haste. These,(the papers they asked for), were declared not sufficient. This was done at least three times. In addition, several calls were made by the designated social worker to satisfy the different requirements that arose each week that I went in to the office in an attempt to register to enter the program. These attempts stretched over a six-week period. Not bad for a simple sign in procedure. One that should have taken about ten minutes.

After the sixth week of run around, I displayed a little frustration and asked the receptionist why it took so long for a court appointed person to enroll in an on-going class. She advised me that she would bypass all the remaining hurdles and enroll me beginning the next Saturday. This she did. My paper had the wrong date on it and I missed the first session. The date was rescheduled for the next Saturday. I paid for an extra session. The first session went well, I thought.

During the second session, I was told that this class was probably not for me. I was asked what I could possibly learn. My answer was, maybe there are a few new laws or methods that I don't know about. Anyway a review is always helpful. I told her that there was another class that I could take but I had chosen this one. This is the one that I would take. The third session, the teacher did not show. The next several weeks, seven to be exact, a different reason was given every week as to why my third intake session was not given. When I challenged their program as to it seeming to not want me in their program, I was assigned a counseling session immediately.

When I arrived at the session, I was told that I could not stay in that session. I complained again and was given a private session. It cost me an extra five dollars. During this third session, I was also advised that this class may not be for me. At this third intake session, I was assigned a class. When I arrived in the class, I was asked to leave. I was asked by that teacher to call another person and attend her class. I called this teacher and was told that I could not attend her class. When I talked to the receptionist this time, she said that the director was out of town and would resolve this latest matter when they returned.

My first session was two weeks later. I was the only Afro American in the class. I was openly challenged every session until the tenth session. After the second session, four men came to me after the class and advised me to say exactly what the teachers told me to say or they would not let me pass the class. They felt that I was being targeted by the teachers for some unknown reason. In the tenth session, I spoke of the reason why I took a time out every day instead of one practice time out a week as the class suggested or when anger came upon us. Several of the persons in the class adopted this practice.

This did not set well with the instructors. It seemed that I had triumphed over their basic instruction. In the fifteenth session, a new

107

instructor came in. We were given three to five minutes to state our assignment. He challenged me three times in the first minute and a half. It was done in an extremely hostile argumentative manner. On the last session, number sixteen, he told me that I had not turned in my homework and that I would be given a half miss.

This was an open lie. Not only had I turned in my homework for the session but also I had given those who had not done their homework for that session, the questions before going into the class. The homework only took about five minutes to do. No one especially me leaves their homework undone. I did mine the week before and put it in my folder as usual. At the end of the session at week sixteen, the teacher advised me that he had only been in two sessions but did not feel that I had fulfilled the goal of the class and needed more skills as taught by the class. A total of one year training to be exact. This was to me a great observation since I had spoken less than ten minutes in those two classes. Also because I was the only one that he advised had to do a repeat, especially a full year on the basis of two five minute talks. The talks were on an incident in our lives. Each person was allowed three to five minutes to participate.

Again the contents of the class that he was attempting to teach had been taught by me for over the past nine years. Similar contents are included in my regular family training and counseling classes. I taught three day sessions three times a year at that time and at various seminars around the country. I am quite certain that he was not aware that I had taught these things to both men and women for over fifteen years at that time. Nor was he aware that the two or three minute principal to promote a thought that I taught during these years to so many others was carefully followed during these times. I am certain that he was not aware that over thirty-five nationalities had been taught these principles by myself.

My teaching so many nationalities was one of my primary reasons for staying current on children connected health and safety laws at that time. I am quite certain that from the beginning, I was targeted as an undesirable in this CHD program in San Jose, California. I refused to bow out. I do not believe that the initial delays, the non-show classes and the initial advice that this class may not be for me along with the challenges in every class but two was accidental. I consider my treatment in this CHD program some of the most blatant racism that I have experienced in my over forty years of public activities. Time and time again some of the men in this class expressed to me that whatever it takes to obtain their children or to reunite them with their families, they would do it. If they had to be a parrot, they would be. These men considered their children and families as being used as Hostages. Their mouth was sealed and the teachers had the key.

No program has the right to deliberately refuse, hinder, harass, humiliate, or misrepresent the facts of ones attendance and participation in any program funded in part with City, County, State, or Federal funds. Especially one recommended so highly by the courts. Who dares to complain when the weight of the judicial system appears to be against them? As one employee was overheard as she spoke to a man complaining about his scheduling. The courts sent you here. It is your problem to comply.

To take from February to April to enroll a person in a simple sign here and enter the ongoing class is bad enough.   Now let us think seriously. In a five-minute talk would you expect to be challenged no matter what you say? Compare your sayings with everyone else and find that no matter how similar they are, you are the one that is challenged. Consider one instructor's statement to me. I don't care what the law says. In this class you say and do what we say. This is all that matters. Is there a court ordered class that can ignore the law and be justified?

Now compound matters a little. Enter two sessions that you were sent to by the courts and find yourself being asked to leave or hear the suggestion to not attend. Compound a little more. Be advised to enter another teacher's class and be told that you cannot come in here. Go a little further. Meet a teacher that you have never seen before and hear him speak with an attitude in a negative fashion as you began your five-minute speech. Listen to the conclusion as you are told that you need to take a years training to get you out of your rut. Your attitude needs to be revamped.

Now consider all of this when you have been teaching people from thirty different countries these same values for over nine years and general family values for over fifteen years. Consider that every family session that I taught was an ask a question at any time during the session class. As the instructor said. What can you learn? You know too much. Maybe this class is not for you. Was this a compliment or a warning? Stay away. We don't want you. You will pay dearly if you come in. This is a CHD program that I will never forget. It is also one that I will never recommend without an attitude change. Let those with knowledge in this valley cry loudly *** let my people go ***

A few years ago I entered a government facility and went through a briefing. I heard that six young men were unwelcome residents and their actions were to be observed, noted, and no effort be made to encourage their stay. They were targeted to be expelled if possible. Upon noting that five of the six were black, I chose to seek them out and find out their problems. To my surprise, only one of the young men had a problem. He had lied about his age. He was under age for this facility. With less than ten minutes counseling with each student, each one finished their two- year schooling with flying colors and one in particular became a great inspiration to his fellow students in their mini crisis. Why the turn around? My supervisor told me that he was literally afraid to talk to the black students. He did not know how to deal with them. Ten minutes of counseling offered five students two years of free schooling and meaningful careers. The sixth student got the same opportunity two years later. The supervisor, six years later with a promotion under his belt during that time is still The Center of Civil Rights and Racial Controversy.

Give your child more than counseling. Give your child their Civil Rights. Give them their chance to succeed under a parent's direction. Let your child see a hero and not a coward. Teach them by your example that they cannot only look to a President or Governor but that they can be a President or a Governor. This book was rewritten to give every American Parent a tool to fight for your child. The land of liberty must never be known around the world as The Land Of Hostage Children And Helpless Parents.

Your children are authors, inventors, teachers, explorers, artists, firemen, legislators, lawyers, and doctors. Your job is to provoke them to good works; to inspire them to strive to be successful. Your child will inspire the world when you are gone. Their life is only an extension of your own. Be a world changer. Be a deliverer for your children. You wear the armor. You voice the protest. You surround your child with love, honor, and your sacrifice and your determination. Be a parent. Take charge of your children.

These are real stories. These are real people. This is a real system. This is a part of real America. Are you a real American that will live The Constitution Of America and teach your child to one day be an example of The America that our nation's founders and forefathers intended? Family Civil Rights is guaranteed by The Constitution Of The United States Of America. There is no fee for your Civil Rights to be investigated. Don't let your child become an innocent prisoner of the state. Be a parent.

> Foster care used to always seem to me,
> like a substitute mom or teacher.
> It is not my job, you are sick today.
> I am only here for today's feature.
>
> I don't want your job. I will be your help.
> You will be back on the job tomorrow.
> Your house will be clean and your beds made.
> Coming home will be joy and not sorrow.
>
> I remember the days you carried your child.
> You were big, fat and couldn't tie your shoe.
> You still managed a sometime smile.
> You, cooking in a hot kitchen? That was abuse.
>
> You carried your child for nine long months.
> You suffered nausea, discomfort and pain.
> How can America, look the other way?
> While taking your child away in shame.

22.FOSTER CARE RAPE OF THE AMERICAN FAMILY **** NO RETURN BY LAW.

What do you mean? If your child can be kept in Foster Care Custody for fifteen out of twenty two months, the child may be put up for adoption. Don't become relaxed because your relative is allowed to keep your child in Foster Care. You may be the parent but your child's attachment to the care provider is considered in some counties as a measure of whether or not your child will be returned to you or given to the care giver as an adopted child or long term permanent placement. Is this Anti American? Yes.

No county or state law supported and pushed by the local court system has the authority to violate A Parents Civil Rights as to raising their children. At the same time that The Foster Child is taken into custody some counties are allowed by their County Court System to look for an adoption family at the same time. Your question is did you place my children with A Genuine Foster Care Parent or with an Adoption Searching Family?

THE TELEPHONE CALL

My children had been kept hostages for one year in Jefferson County Colorado. I received a telephone call by a person who had just left family court. "Reverend Andrews?" "Yes this is he." "Do you know that there is no intention to return your children to you?" "I felt that was the case because of all the effort to retain them." "Do you know their intention?"

"Well I have never fully understood why they have tried so hard to discredit me after one year of fight." "I felt that one year is too late to start an investigation on why they kept my children hostage so long." "Reverend, believe me they are going to find some reason." "Why should they when there is no valid reason?" "Twisted words Reverend, twisted words." "A debater is not interested in truth." "Only in coming out as the winner." "They are going to adopt your girls out if they can." "Is that the law? Yes, as long as they have a judge that will go along with whatever the Human Resource Office wants." "Is that legal?" "A judge cannot be touched as far as lawsuits, etc. are concerned." "If they are slanted, that is better than saying crooked." "You can be prosecuted but the judge can't be."

"Preacher, read the county code on adoption" "They can adopt your children out and change their name and social security number while sealing their records." "You told me that they were attempting to brainwash your children to get them to stay in Foster Care some time ago, right?" "Yes." "Operating on their six month system they can easily stage review after review on any frivolous statement or charge as long as a judge goes along with them"

"Remember that the most overturned appeals court in the nation is in California." "They have never removed the judges." "They have only made appeals." "They can and will postpone and delay your children's return because by my information, they want to adopt your girls out." "If the Jefferson County Human Welfare Social Services can keep your children in their care for another few months, you will never see your children again." "It only takes fifteen months of Foster Care Custody with twenty two months of control for you to lose your children forever to a county or state system in America." "This is according to the Children's Code from this county." "This is not illegal prisons overseas." "This is Legal Prisons In America with innocent children as hostages and parents as victims that are unable to provide the ten thousand dollar lawyer fees to fight the case."

"The information that you have given me to date has been right on and never in error." "Yet, I still do not know who I am talking to." "That's all right preacher." "I work in Colorado but all of us here do not go along with this system" Consider this. "Our jobs, our homes and families, even our lives are at stake if we openly work to derail the unfairness of The Foster Care and The Adoption System." <u>You may be too naïve to know it, but</u>

you have made yourself a target of our court system." "You can expect to be made a criminal if it is in any way possible." "You are interfering with millions of dollars." "You have become a crusader in an area of drugs, judges, social workers, bribes, politicians, criminals, and courts." "It is not just your family being liberated. You are a threat to so many that make a living preying on your child while daring you to speak out." "Watch your back. Stay innocent of wrong. Expect an attempt to be made to put you in some way at the mercy of the court system as a common criminal" "Hey, I didn't know that my stand as a father meant so much."

"Use your bible knowledge Reverend" "The man that translated the King James Bible was chased all over Europe to keep him from completing a work that would give all men more truth." "Smile preacher. One of your tapes got to this man from Colorado." "You also said David's mother was a slave and his dad was surprised that God chose him to be king." "I am not surprised at you being a dad." "I have met three of your children." "We don't have kings." "We have governors and presidents." "And Reverend, if you want to know how much your case has stirred the waters in some areas, ask yourself; how much will a person that cannot have a child pay to adopt one?" "Ten thousand dollars is a low figure." "Think higher. There are millions on the line."

I always thought life was fair.
Then my brother set me straight.
 We often walked three miles to school.
We had to be there at half past eight.

We walked through snow that was ankle deep.
In places it was above our knees.
The school bus passed with laughing kids and
 no desire to pick us up even if we said please

There were no hidden accusations.
We all knew where everyone stood.
Contracts were sealed with a handshake.
Honesty and truth were as it should

Lies were not told to win any case.
All men relished a true neighbor.

Justice and honor walked hand in hand.
No one sought the grim reaper's favor

 My brother led through many snowdrifts.
They often came above his waist.
I was always behind walking in his footsteps.
Now I am the leader. I have taken his place.

The bus has passed us many times in the past,
 In snowdrifts with children behind me.
As I approach the school door. It is open.
Thank God almighty, our children are free.

23. THE ADOPTION RACKET **
IN YOUR COUNTY, YOUR STATE, YOUR AMERICA.

Efforts to adopt a child out or to place a child with a legal guardian can be made at the same time attempts are supposedly being made to unify a family. *** Your question should be *** is my child in foster care or in adoption waiting? <u>How can you attempt to return a child to his family and adopt him out at the same time?</u> By a county saying the court is the final decision maker it is attempting to circumvent The Constitutional Civil Rights. A Civil Rights Lawsuit can cost seventy thousand dollars and up. If a person cannot afford five thousand dollars to hire a family lawyer, and another five thousand dollars to file the appeal that he will be forced to file, how can he afford seventy thousand to fight A Civil Rights Case? The judge cannot be sued. The poor man is the only person being exploited.

The adoption kick back is enormous and often very profitable if you go through the official black market door. That door is called unlawful and criminal. Is there another way? Ask the young man that was explaining to his friend that they had no problem getting a child for adoption because his wife talked to the girl in The Foster Care Office. He broke no county laws, while reaching for another dad's child. What if you could stand in line and receive a tearful mother's child while fully protected by the court system?

I once sat in a courtroom and heard the judge say to a distraught mother, this young man is going to a beautiful home. He has a lot of out doors on his ranch and many fine opportunities. The only answer the mother could afford to give; both physically and financially was this answer. Yes but he won't have his loving mom. She did not have funds to hire a lawyer and the lawyer supplied by the court only announced his name and the case he was supposed to represent and sat down. This tearful mother watched her son being taken from her and given to another. This bleeding heart will always cover that judge in blood. Her court appointed lawyer will always be held accountable by the Eternal God for helping to destroy and not unify a family.

How can our nation continue to grow when we despise, belittle, and destroy our own families under the guise that An Adoptive or Foster Parent is better loving than A Parent. Our Nation's Civil Rights Code says The Family is the strength of our nation and every effort must be made to strengthen and unify the family. Why have we allowed a county to write a law that is a blueprint to invade every home at will on any allegation made by any social worker who is supported by a yes man judge? Yes, you say it and I will do it judge.

If your child is 12 years or older and refuses to go along with the program, their law states that they must be counseled by a professional with knowledge about adoption, teens and permanency placement. Why? Because they must say yes to the adoption to make it legal according to (their) written law. What does this mean? The child will be subjected to America's legal brainwashing technique for children. The most popular system term or name for this is called therapy. Their aim is to persuade the child to say yes to the adoption or the placement program for them at that time. If your child has been in the adoptive home for a year, the county must request from the court that the adoption be expedited. Where are the parents? Totally silenced by the court.

The Parents Rights must be terminated by The County before they can adopt your child out. The county makes the charge and the judge of their choice makes the approval. Your child is then given a new ID, a new name, new social security number and a new authority in their life. They will never have a new mother or father but your life with your children will be history.

117

You will never again parent that child per America's Legal, Family Rape System. Mother and father contact with your children will no longer be permitted by the system. The county accuse, the court approve, the chosen persons receive. Is this the freedom to raise your child and family that was and is envisioned by our constitutional civil rights? Did the founders of our country envision a dictatorship that denied family training, education, religion, and jobs, etc by American parents? Did they envision putting family control in the hands of a county vigilante system operated by a county court system that refuses to allow the residents to direct their own lives? Did you elect your officials to control your children and to legislate every parent to the position of a mindless zombie? Or did you elect them to provide direction for your environment as you and your family live in the pursuit of life, liberty, and happiness?

Your Foster Care Adopted Child that has been taken from a parent's home is not dying on a battlefield across the world. They are being trained in another family's bed while a poor mother or father is bending their head in grief and wringing their hands in sorrow. Their hair is gray before its time and the wrinkles in their face is the signature of grief. A broken heart is not fixed by seeing an empty chair that your child once sat on. Ask the thousands that have had their homes raided on assumptions and untrue allegations. Ask the thousands that have been told that you made one wrong turn and ran one red light so I will never let you forget it.

Why have America not raised a cry against the Foster Care Adoption Racket Home Invasion Practice? One reason *** the parents are often belittled, embarrassed, humiliated with the accusations, and too poor to afford the lawyer to fight the case. They are too fearful that their children will not be returned at all. All too often that is the case. What should the poor do? Fight anyhow. Dial the toll free Civil Rights cry. The poor are again exploited for the desires of those that appear more affluent. The strength of the poor lies in one word. Numbers! If those that have lost children to this manipulation will rise as a unit, America will hold to the law and once more stand on The Constitution Of The United States Of America as far as families is concerned.

We often talk of the great men of old that put their life on the line in biblical days. We talk of Moses, and Jesus who put their life on the line to deliver God's people. We honor their lives because they stood for honor, freedom, and justice.

Have we forgotten the blood of those in American history that gave themselves for our family freedoms? Do we remember the blood of Rodolfo Gonzales, Daniel Imouye, Lucretia Mott, Abraham Lincoln, Frederick Douglas, Maggie Kuhn, Dennis Banks, Mike Masoka, Jane Adams, Eleanor Roosevelt, Martin Luther King, Betty Friedan, Ceasar Chavez, and Rosa Parks. These are only a few that have stood in time past for the diverse families of America. Indians, Blacks, Japanese, Women, Mexicans, and others of America's heritage.

How can our present day America allow all of these efforts of people we call great be destroyed by simply turning our heads and allowing our children to be taken captive at will?

Today it is our children. Tomorrow it will be our women and the next day our men. These will wake up in The Lions Den or The American Roman Arena fighting for their lives. Fighting against not a fleshly beast but a system beast that has become the system dictator. Not a single man or woman, but a system that has us in bondage. Can America break this bondage?

The Adoption Assistance and Child Welfare Act of 1980 requires that each state make reasonable efforts to prevent out of home placements and to reunify the family when appropriate. Health and safety are major concerns. This Federal Law also requires that every state and local elected official along with lawyers, judges, attorneys, guardians and ad-litems take the responsibility that these laws be implemented.

The Children's Code expressly states that prior to adoption, the child can be left in the custody of the other parent. The other parent can expect to be bombarded with allegations and accusations by the county or its agents if their intention is to keep the child for the maximum time that the government will pay them or if they have an adoptive family in mind. If your child is unfortunate enough to be placed in an adoptive home, this can result in a greater problem because their attachment to the caregiver is considered in the adoption or placement process. A person looking to keep your child will work harder to persuade the child. Consider that the caregiver's self serving efforts and the trained professional that has a job to persuade your child to accept adoption is great pressure on a child separated from his family and among strangers. It is akin to legal slavery or solicitation of a minor into crime. The child is too immature to resist properly.

The federal law was never intended to be used in this manner. Yet it is. You can stop this at your door. Unfortunately if the parent's rights have been terminated prior to this adoption process, the parent will not even know that his child has been adopted nor where he is after the adoption. Your door begins when the hostage takers arrive. And remember *** it is illegal to persuade a child to not return to their parents according to the Civil Rights Law.

24. DECLARE THE PARENT MENTALLY UNFIT * PUT THE PARENT IN CONTEMPT OF COURT ** DOCUMENTARY

A few days after my Colorado call, I was advised by my home state that another home study was asked for to verify my ability to raise my children. I was asked three times, would I object to taking a psychological evaluation. My answer was repeated to me so the questioner was certain that I said I would not consent to such for the return of my children. In the meantime I had obtained a letter from the Hostage State asking why a psychological evaluation had been requested from my home state. I had been told by my home state that the Hostage State had asked for the evaluation. A few days later I received a letter from the Hostage State requesting such an evaluation.

Prior to receiving the letter, I was able to obtain a report from the Hostage State saying I was suspected of having mental problems. The Hostage State said that my home state had stated that I was suspected of having mental problems. The report said someone would be staffed to handle this. I began looking forward to being assaulted and accused now on a mental level. This was extremely important to me because both my home state and the Hostage Taker State had both accused each other of requesting the evaluation.

My conclusion was that both were conspiring together because I had challenged the system ** or that my home state had effectively bowed out of the dispute by asking me what I would not agree to and then suggesting

121

and implementing it. I also obtained another report saying that I could not take care of all of my children together. This came from the Hostage State of Colorado. I wonder who submitted that report. The report said that someone would be assigned to take care of the problem. Being a good parent can be a problem to an abuser of the American Peoples Civil Rights. I remembered my secret informer's statement. They will make you a criminal. The home study supervisor said the psycho exam is part of a court order. My refusing to take it put me in contempt of court. Is family freedom worth such a label? YES, YES, YES.

Freedom from tyranny and oppression of the American People is the foundation of this American Republic. If our American ways, laws, and practices, freely assault our American Families: if our American Children are taken hostage at will and our parents voices silenced; what is the difference in a presidential dictator and a court system dictator? Our children are our future. A family threat is a national threat. Rome did not fall in a day. The government fell into corruption a little at a time.

Ask yourself if the invasion of our Family Civil Rights is the beginning of a plan to control your entire life? Is this the beginning of an anarchy of control that is not from a man but from a partially out of control Family Court System? Is this a system that will make every family a slave and every one of its employees a junior tyrant enforcing the will of a dictator or a system?

Let our families relish the independence that made America great from the beginning. To search for a word to justify one's self says that my works were not enough to impress my onlookers. To live a life dedicated to freedom of your children will enable you to stand with Washington and his little poorly clothed, hungry army. The only thing they appeared to be big in was a desire to be free from tyranny and be men and women of a great free nation. They wanted to dream their own dreams, plan their own future and build their own families. You are the children of that rag tag, freedom-loving army. Your children are the grand children of that rag tag army. It was able to challenge the world's greatest power for the freedom to live as God ordained. It won. It triumphed in the face of all odds.

We will raise our families in love, joy, and peace fully protected by The Constitution Of The United States Of America. Our Civil Rights have been fought and died for. We will not surrender them. We will purge the cancers and heal the wounds. We shall sing that this is Our America The Beautiful. Our land of the free; Our home of the brave; Your America; Your freedom; Your home; the greatest free nation on earth. Not the greatest oppressor of our own families. We shall maintain our freedom in the face of all odds. Both from without and from within, we will not allow our children to become Hostages Of The State anymore. They will not be innocent prisoners without a trial from this day forth.

**** memories **** true memories *** memories ****
One of the surveys that came into my hands around 1960 stated that nine out of ten of the people that were in mental institutions at that time were there because of religious problems. Was the lord trying to have revival and preachers were rebelling? Or was there a wholesale attack on those preaching the soon return of Christ Jesus at that time?

**** memories ** true memories ***

Pappy was a coal miner. He was living common law with one of the local women. Pappy was a rather quiet man. There was no television in this area at that time. The only entertainment was the radio. Pappy could be found at times entertaining some of the youngsters with a few old time folk songs. Some of them he made up himself. A couple of times a month, pappy and his common law wife would be found engaging in the usual Friday night village family squabble. What was that? Arguing over the paycheck. At that time, our state had a rather well known law. It was seldom used in our area because we knew everyone for miles around and anyone that dared use it became an outcast. One day Pappy became quite irritated and ran down the country road with his lunch box. Only four black families lived in this area. Pappy was black. We did not hear from Pappy for a few weeks.

Our state had a law at that time that if you suspected a person of being mentally ill you could call the mental institution and they would pick the person up or the local police would do it for them. The local police in our area at that time was about twenty miles away. Someone had called and reported Pappy as being mentally ill. He was picked up and taken to the state mental institution. He never returned home. He died in the institution. I was able to visit Pappy once when a delegation of the black

123

families went to see him. I saw not a vibrant pappy but a zombie living in an institute where people are often spaced out on drugs. A couple of years later, this state actually paid each person that put a person in this system. How long did this last? Until it was discovered that a certain rich man was being held as a medicated patient. This law was changed because of one rich man. It was not changed for Pappy. He was only a poor black man. Why would another poor black man volunteer to reinvent a system that had destroyed his neighbor and his friend? I have not forgotten.

** experience **

one year ago, I was called and asked to go to a hospital. A person had been placed in the mental ward. The social worker was considering placing the person in a locked facility. I was called prior to the worker obtaining the court order to do so. The patient was released to me and has had no more problems while maintaining their own apartment. About five years ago a patient was committed to this facility and did enter into a locked mental facility for a period of one year. The patient was released into my custody and has managed to maintain an almost normal life. No parent needs a psycho evaluation to see if he can be a parent. My experience and I have only given you a couple of about thirty plus would never approve or advise such. How anxious is the county to control the parents of the children they take away???? I believe I read that anyone that had contact with the minor in the home, babysitter, live in persons, other parent, grandparents, can be named as respondents. **** Is that serious? ****

It is when the code says that from the time you are notified, you are subject to that Court System. When the code says that the court can name anyone it thinks it should as a respondent. Remember, this is not guilty as per say, but thinks one may be per say. Such a code is a danger to our society. It destroys the only accuse and prosecute the guilty part of the law. It removes the innocent until proven guilty concept. It can name anyone a suspect or respondent. Look a little further. It can impose conditions upon the respondent that can create a transgression of the law or make a person an implied offender.

What about my children? No, not my personal children! Ask yourself, what about my children? Your children!

My children are innocent. They are innocent today. Will they remain free or will they become Hostages, Prisoners Of The State? Will my sons and daughters be denied their parental rights? Will my country become a system-oriented dictator? Can I believe the law will mean what it says when I Stand before a judge?****** <u>let us give these Innocent Prisoners Without A Trial their God Given Right to America's Freedom. These are My Children. These are the world changers of today and tomorrow. Doctors, lawyers, scientists, teachers, clergy, sports, entertainers, these are our children. Set them free. Keep them free.</u>

As I was completing this manuscript, a cry was raised about suspected terrorists being held prisoners in foreign countries. Someone had the boldness to rattle the halls of congress and seek to set our Whitehouse on what they thought to be the right track. Our policy is to not negotiate with terrorists. America considers them a threat to our freedom. ****

Our children are not a threat to our nation. They are not terrorists. Still they are being taken from parents by the thousands and held hostage. Many are held in secret homes. Ask your social worker where their Assigned Children Hostages are living. If they are not with a relative, where are they? Are they hidden from society or from the parent? They may not be suffering torture but they certainly are being trained by another trainer beside a parent.

How many new things have you been accused of since your child has been a Hostage. One man said if you do that again I will have your hide. A mother was quoted as saying, I will skin you alive. Neither of these statements posed a danger to the children. Neither parent should have been cited for child endangerment. This was their normal household conversation. This is a freedom loving America, I hope. Their children should be returned to such an one. Why do they still remain in an American Prison that is tailored especially for children.

Foster Care or Foster Prison. Adoption Elect or Adoption Kidnap. Innocent Prisoners Without A Trial. How did over <u>five hundred and fifteen thousand of our children get into Foster Care</u> according to my figures at the time of this writing? Why are these figures kept secret? <u>How</u>

did it occur that over Sixty (60%) percent of these children are suspect of being removed illegally from the parent's home? Why is there a blackout concerning the custody of these children? How many will be brainwashed against their families and be retrained? How many will be farmed out to adoption families while their parents walk in sorrow and shed tears daily? Germany's Jews began by wearing a star as a mandatory requirement. They continued by being forced to live in ghettos. Their destination next became prison camps. They ended up in fiery furnaces and mass graves. They were purged by a system that took control of their homes and families. Consider how innocent protecting the children sounds.

Look at the destination by today's statistics. See how thousands are ending up! The unemployment rate in some areas has been reported as high as forty percent among Former Foster Care Children. One major prison counts its population as high as 70% being Former Foster Care Persons. This represents Foster Care System Failure. This system was originally not intended to be a family ruler or family dictator. It was never intended to be a suppressor of every families Civil Rights,***** or was this the plan all along? Is this agency a government sponsored road to dictator over every American? One major communist spoke in the 1940's that they only needed one generation to conquer America, if only they could reach our youth. Is The Human Resource Youth, Family and Children Services along with Social Welfare and Child Protective Services the vehicle that will accomplish this hidden goal of a few in America? (To reach our youth to corrupt their morals?) Is this the future of our children?

No system ever has or ever will surpass parental authority and parental control of their own homes and families. Parents Civil Rights must be restored and protected in our families. The Child's Civil Rights must be protected for they are our heritage and future. America belongs to us and our children. Family Civil Rights are a part of Our Constitution. In only twenty-five years the act signed in 1980 to shield our children has been twisted to appear as a prison instead of a door to freedom. What was designed and promoted to become a road to protection is in many ways being manipulated to become a road to A Hostage Of The State for our children with the parents placed on parole.

I call on every parent to raise your voice on behalf of You And Your Child's Civil Rights. Stand before the lawmakers and authorities until both you and your children are released within the borders of the life, liberty, hope and freedom that made America great. You and I should and must have the freedom to shape our destiny without any government interference in our pursuit of life, liberty and happiness. Let not one day pass without every parent knocking on the judge's door until you and your child are known by name across America. Your cry must be for freedom to raise your child as a free American without state or government control. You are your child's teacher, and mentor. Let freedom ring and set your child free. <u>Why should your child be A Hostage Of The State in a free America?</u>

Thanks